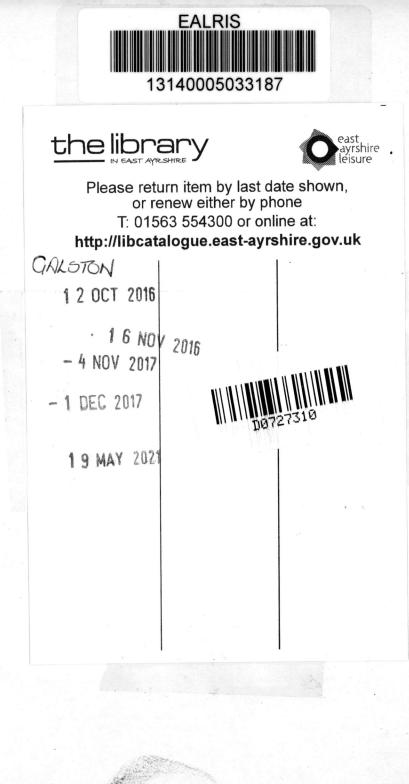

Linda Blair is an Associate Fellow of the British Psychological Society, a Chartered Scientist and is registered with the Health Professions Council. She has worked as a clinical psychologist for over 30 years. She has written advice columns for the *Guardian* and *The Times*, and for *Psychologies* and *Junior* magazines. Linda also appears frequently on television and radio.

The
Key
to
Calm

Your Path to Mindfulness – and Beyond

Linda Blair

First published in Great Britain in 2014 by Yellow Kite Books
An imprint of Hodder & Stoughton
An Hachette UK company

1

A CIP catalogue record for this title is available from the British Library

Trade Paperback ISBN 978 1 444 76534 2
eBook ISBN 978 1 444 76535 9

Printed and bound by Clays Ltd, St Ives plc

Hodder & Stoughton policy is to use papers that are natural, renewable and recyclable products and made from wood grown in sustainable forests. The logging and manufacturing processes are expected to conform to the environmental regulations of the country of origin.

Hodder & Stoughton Ltd
338 Euston Road
London NW1 3BH

www.hodder.co.uk

For Rob

Contents

Introduction

Stress levels today are unacceptably high. For example, in 2011–2012, 40 per cent of all work-related illnesses in the UK – that's more than 420,000 cases – were stress-related. Our worries about finance and job security mean that 'stress' has become the most common reason for long-term sick leave in the UK today. Those who work in the caring professions – nurses and teachers, for example – appear to be some of the hardest hit. Worryingly, no one seems to know when things might improve.

At the same time, the number of treatments available to alleviate stress, the number of books available to teach you how to beat stress, and the number of medications designed to dampen the symptoms of stress, are all increasing rapidly.

It sounds like nothing much is helping and no one's getting better. So what's going wrong?

The answer is fairly simple. No one has yet approached the problems we face today in the right way.

Stress is nothing new. Humans have endured enormous pressure at other times in the past, during times of international conflict for example, and we've coped remarkably well. However, what's different today is that we're seldom presented with only one challenge at a time. Today, we're almost always asked to face multiple challenges and to deal with them simultaneously.

Furthermore, everything seems to be changing faster than ever before. It feels that as soon as we master one system or technique, another comes along to replace it. No living creature finds rapid change easy and human beings, with our delicately sensitive and complex brains, find the readjustment particularly stressful.

The change from relatively quiet surroundings to a '24/7 buzz' is very recent, so recent that it's occurred within living memory for many of us. James Herriot, the author and Yorkshire vet, recounts a charming example of 'technology free living' in his book *It Shouldn't Happen to a Vet*, when he is asked to visit the Bramleys, a family of three brothers and their sister, all middle-aged and single. Their isolated farm had no modern amenities, not even a radio or TV. The family worked hard and lived simply. This is what Herriot found when he finally reached the farm house:

'I was about to knock when I stopped with my hand poised. I found I was looking through the kitchen window and in

the interior, dimly lit by an oil lamp, the Bramleys were sitting in a row.'

'*They weren't grouped round the fire but were jammed tightly on a long, high-backed wooden settle which stood against the far wall. The strange thing was the almost exact similarity of their attitudes; all four had their arms folded, chins resting on their chests, feet stretched out in front of them. The men had removed their heavy boots and were stocking-footed, but Miss Bramley wore an old pair of carpet slippers.'*

'*I stared, fascinated by the curious immobility of the group. They were not asleep, not talking or reading or listening to the radio – in fact they didn't have one – they were just sitting.'*

'Just sitting'. When did you last find time just to sit? Nowadays, no one feels they're allowed to be relaxed and idle – just to sit. The result of this increasingly complex, rapidly changing environment is that we've begun to feel so overwhelmed that we're often unable to think clearly or to make decisions – in effect, we simply freeze, not knowing where to turn next. Nowadays, not only are many of us plagued by the usual symptoms of stress – breathlessness and restlessness, an inability to sleep well or to concentrate – now we are often gripped by a sense of total paralysis, unable to make any decisions and not knowing where to turn. One of my patients described this as 'feeling like a rabbit, frozen in the headlights.' And yet, despite this new picture of stress, experts are trying to deal with our reaction to it in the same old ways.

Some of the methods target isolated symptoms rather than considering the whole person. So for example, there are all sorts of treatments available to help tackle insomnia or to teach us all how to overcome negative thinking which are no doubt helpful in a limited way. The problem, however, is that treating only the symptoms means that we continue to overlook the central mechanisms that are generating them.

Other experts offer a single panacea, one overall approach that's meant to cure all ills. Cognitive therapy and positive thinking are good examples. Although these treatments are very helpful, their scope is limited. On their own, they're not enough. Human problems are too complex to be eliminated with one bullet, even a silver one.

Finally, there are those who treat stress by masking symptoms medicinally or by teaching sufferers how to eliminate bad habits. But these are only half solutions. If an individual isn't taught what to do when the medication is stopped, or what to replace bad habits with, chances are that sooner or later, the bad habits will creep back.

The time has come for something fresh and new. What we need now is a holistic approach, a method that can be integrated into the lives we're living today. What we really need, in fact, is a treatment that *becomes* the way we live now.

That's what *The Key to Calm* offers you. I know it's

effective, because I've been using it at my clinics for years now and I've seen the results. The Five Step programme you'll learn about in this book is the result of 33 years of clinical practice.

When I first began seeing patients, I focused entirely on their problems. Together, we worked out ways to overcome bad habits, and to eliminate negative thoughts and beliefs. After all, that's what I understood to be the role of a clinical psychologist. In terms of getting rid of negativity, my approach definitely helped. However, the help was often only temporary. I now realise that getting rid of what's causing distress should only be the start of a programme that is designed to create true psychological health. Unless you build good habits to replace the bad, and unless you work to improve *all* important aspects of daily living, it's all too easy, once treatment stops, for an individual to fall back onto their older, destructive ways of living.

Therefore, rather than simply offer treatments that eliminate problems, what I now believe is that it's necessary also to offer a better way of living, a positive way forward that takes into account all aspects of a fulfilling life. *The Key to Calm* is that better way.

WHO THIS BOOK IS INTENDED TO HELP

This book is *not* intended to cure acute psychological illness. No book can do that on its own. If you're suffering from a diagnosable psychological condition – clinical depression or an obsessive compulsive disorder, for example – then you should see your GP so you can get the professional help you both need and deserve.

If, however, you have suffered from a psychological disorder in the past and are now recovered, and you want to do all you can to make sure you don't relapse, then this book will help you. If you've never suffered a psychological illness but worry that your lifestyle is making you vulnerable to such problems, then again, this book will help you. And if you're one of the millions today who often feel overwhelmed and over-stressed, and you believe there's a better way to cope with the current speed of change and the multiple demands that are so often made on us, then this book is exactly what you need.

Once the five steps are incorporated into your life – once, that is, they become the way you approach each day – you'll no longer worry about whether you'll be able cope when you face new challenges. Instead, you'll find that in fact you start to welcome challenge. You'll know yourself better, you'll become more aware of what's happening around you, and you'll enjoy your life more.

The Five Step programme is presented simply. It's sensible and practical, and you can get started using it right away. Furthermore, the positive effects are cumulative. The more steps you incorporate into your life and the longer you live in this new way, the calmer, more balanced and more contented you will become.

Here's a brief description of each of the five steps:

Step One: Stop, Look and Listen

The first and most important step is to stop trying to defend against everything that's going on *without* – that is, in your current environment. These are circumstances you can't often change anyway. Instead, you need to begin by regaining your *inner* balance and your ability to focus. You'll do this by learning to become mindful, to regain the ability to concentrate and to focus fully and non-judgementally on what's happening right now.

Step Two: Take Care of Your Best Asset

The best way to adapt to change and to solve new problems is to start with the healthiest body and mind possible. In this step, you'll be offered the most up-to-date information about physical health and psychological wellbeing, so you can learn how to take the best possible care of your mind and body.

Step Three: Know Yourself

One of the reasons we've become more vulnerable today is that we undervalue ourselves and underestimate our potential. In this step you'll gain a much clearer idea of who you are, of your personality profile and your intellectual strengths and weaknesses. I'll also teach you how to rediscover your own deep-seated passions and enthusiasms.

Step Four: Streamline Your Life

In this step you'll learn how to 'declutter' – in other words, how to simplify your life so you can feel clear-minded, balanced and ready to embrace challenge. You'll learn to declutter psychologically, to get rid of the negative core beliefs that may be holding you back. You'll also learn to declutter physically, to simplify your surroundings so you're no longer troubled by unnecessary distractions and so your schedule can open up and allow for things you *really* want to do. I'll teach you how to plan ahead efficiently, and finally, how to say 'no' effectively, so you can feel more in control of your life.

Step Five: Reach Out

Our identity is determined in relation to other people. No matter how able you are to focus, no matter how streamlined your schedule, you'll not feel fully fulfilled and calm unless you spend some time with those who matter most to you. In this fifth step, you'll learn the best ways to build and maintain your relationships.

HOW TO USE THIS BOOK

Start by reading the entire book straight through. Make a note of the sections that stand out, the ones that feel particularly relevant for you.

Then turn back to Step One and start living more mindfully. Stay with this step until it feels like the most natural and comfortable way for you to approach each day. This will take some of you a few days; others will linger longer before moving on to the next step. The important thing is to take the programme at a pace that feels right for you.

Next, choose the step that feels most relevant and important to you when you read the book through initially. Incorporate the guidelines given in that chapter into your daily life, until they, too, feel natural.

Now take another look at the remaining three steps and choose the one you'd like to work on next. Carry on until you've worked through and incorporated all five steps into your daily life – or in other words, until you feel calm, strong and balanced almost all the time.

At that point, you'll realise that you've stopped feeling overloaded and overwhelmed and that you're looking at life in an entirely new way. No longer will you feel afraid when some new problem crops up. Now you'll actually seek out new challenges and meet them head on, confident that you can deal effectively with whatever comes your way.

Before you begin, I'd like to extend my best wishes. I hope that what you learn in this book will provide you with valuable and lasting ways to enrich your life so that you can live as calmly, as fully, and as contentedly as possible.

Step One:
Stop, Look and Listen

'Focus is your strength'
Motto of the Great Britain Paralympic Team 2012

Wouldn't it be wonderful if you could look back on everything you do with pride, knowing that you always give every task and every encounter the greatest care and attention possible? Wouldn't it be lovely to know that you'll never again need to apologise for sloppy work, or for glossing over something you could have done more carefully?

This is exactly what will happen when you live mindfully. That's because when you are mindful – that is, fully focused on the task at hand and not on anything else at that moment – you can be certain that you couldn't have tried harder. You'll know you did the best job you could have done at the time.

When you live mindfully, you'll feel on top of things. Instead of reacting to whatever happens, rushing around trying to please, you'll start to feel in charge. In other words, you'll centre yourself first, take in the current situation, and then, with your attention calmly fixed, decide how best to deal with whatever's going on.

When you are mindful, it feels like you've found the right focus, or the pattern that 'just fits'. It's like turning a kaleidoscope and finding that suddenly, the image is coherent and beautiful. The pieces of colour are all still there just as they've always been, but now the pattern they make looks balanced and attractive.

That's why the first step to regaining your inner calm is to become mindful. Once you've adopted this mind-set, all else will follow. In particular:

- You'll be more aware of yourself physically and of your state of mind, and therefore you'll be in the best position to know how to keep yourself healthy and mentally sound (Step Two).
- You'll be much more aware of your own unique skills and talents, so you can get the best out of yourself and increase your chances of succeeding in whatever you choose to do (Step Three).
- You'll be able to plan more realistically, work more effectively, and avoid taking on too much (Step Four).
- You'll find that you're more interested in what's going on around you, and that you enjoy the time you spend with others more fully (Step Five).

Learning to be mindful will ground you and prepare you for the four steps that follow. This first step, more than any other, offers you the key to calm.

How to make every moment count

Take a moment to stop and reflect – not on what you have to do or have done, but instead on your state of mind. Think about the way you feel as you negotiate your way through your busy day, attempting to juggle the demands of your family and your commitments at work. I expect you feel overwhelmed and at times, even helpless. To make matters worse, you probably also feel sapped of energy. Unless you begin by clearing your mind so that you can regain the ability to make informed choices, anything else I suggest will simply feel like yet another demand on your time, and it will only intensify your distress.

Therefore, the first thing you need to do is to teach yourself to become fully aware of the demands that are made upon you, *without* feeling overwhelmed by them. That's what mindfulness is all about. To borrow the elegant words of Jon Kabat-Zinn, 'Mindfulness means paying attention in a particular way: on purpose, in the present moment, and non-judgmentally' (*Wherever You Go, There You Are*, J. Kabat-Zinn, 1994, p.4).

The secret here is the word 'non-judgmentally'. There are no 'shoulds', no sense of obligation, no wearied push to action. After all, your knee-jerk reactions in the past haven't done you much good, have they? No doubt they've only left you feeling as overwhelmed as ever.

The first step to feeling calm and in control is to learn how to take in whatever is happening fully and calmly, without reacting to it immediately. You also need that initial pause so you have a chance to notice how you are feeling. Only then, when you put the two together, will you be in a position to choose the wisest course of action.

At first, taking the time to be mindful will feel a bit cumbersome, and you may worry that it's costing you too much time. However, once you realise how little time that process actually takes, once you notice how much calmer you feel generally, and once you notice how much better you've become at making good decisions and eliminating mistakes, your discomfort will disappear – in fact, you'll want to be mindful more and more of the time.

Begin taking charge of your life, *right now*. Whenever you feel the obligations piling up, *stop!* Take in the situation fully, give yourself permission to notice what's going on before you start reacting in the tired old ways, and feel the release of tension within you.

Here's an example. The next time someone asks you to join them for a night out, take a moment to reflect before you reply. Do you have other plans already in place, ones you'd have to cancel and perhaps risk hurting someone's feelings or letting people down? Were you planning on having an early night to restore yourself, and without it you know you'll be less effective the next day? If either is true, it would be wise simply to say, 'No, I'm sorry I can't join you this time.' If on the other hand the offer appeals to you and the evening is free, then when you accept, you can do so knowing that you'll be able to enjoy that time with your friend wholeheartedly, without any nagging doubts.

Reflection before action

Perhaps when you were growing up you were told to always trust your intuition – that is, to act on your 'gut instinct' whenever you meet a new challenge. You may be wondering how mindfulness can be compatible with such an attitude.

Mindful awareness doesn't call for you to ignore anything at all. You'll begin to notice everything that's going on in the present moment, and that includes what's happening both within you and around you. Mindful awareness does not, however, include action, and especially not *r*eaction! When you're mindful, you merely observe, valuing everything you notice equally, but acting on nothing immediately. Only after that time of non-judgmental contemplation, only after observing the entire picture, will you choose your response and then act on that choice. The sequence of response that shows most wisdom is this: Use your senses to notice, then use your mind to know. Next, choose a course of action and only then, begin to act.

However, instinct isn't to be undervalued. Immediate reactions are almost always 'correct', in the sense that they're designed to protect you from immediate danger. Intuition is defined as 'the ability to understand or know something immediately, without conscious reasoning' (*Pocket Oxford English Dictionary,* OUP, 2005). If a situation can be responded to emotionally and does not demand any rational input, then of course it will be fine to go ahead and act on your instinct alone in that event.

How often, however, has that been the case in your

experience? Compared to our ancestors we now live in a relatively safe environment, and most things we're required to react to – particularly when we're at work or interacting with friends and family – demand a logical response, rather than an emotional one, requiring you to take some time to make a reasoned assessment before you take action. Just think about the number of times you've fired off an angry email or shouted at someone, and then later you wish you'd taken the time to stop and *think* before you acted. Mindful awareness offers you that window of time. It eliminates the chance that you'll behave in ways you'll regret later.

But what about those situations – however rare they may be – when you're faced with immediate and grave danger? If you take time to notice, then to know, then to reason, wouldn't you put yourself at risk of acting too late?

In cases of real danger, you need to act immediately – and on those rare occasions, you will. There's no need, therefore, to worry about how you'll react to a real threat. The human brain is exquisitely prepared to recognise true and immediate danger. When we're in a truly mortally threatening situation the most primitive part of our brain, the part that's dedicated to survival, takes over immediately and completely. We act at once, either by escaping or attacking. No time is wasted creating an emotional response or registering how we're feeling. Neither does logic kick in – not even a split second is spent choosing between alternative courses of action. We simply act to save ourselves and/or our loved ones.

People who've been in that kind of immediate danger

and survived unscathed will tell you that they didn't feel frightened at the time. In fact, they'll tell you that they weren't aware of feeling anything at all. However, once they're out of danger they may well react emotionally. They may be plagued by panic attacks, distressing flashbacks, and nightmares. This is a condition that's known as PTSD, or Post-Traumatic Stress Disorder.

Bridget is a good example of someone who suffered PTSD. One day when she was walking home from work, she witnessed a terrible accident. A ten year-old boy who was riding his bicycle across the street from her suddenly hit a rock and careened out onto the road. He was hit almost immediately by a car just behind him. Bridget, who was a trained nurse, rushed over and did all she could to revive the child, while another passer-by rang for an ambulance. Despite her best efforts, the boy was pronounced dead when the ambulance arrived.

At the time, Bridget recalled that she wasn't frightened or distressed – in fact, she told me, 'I felt nothing at all, absolutely nothing.' However, about a week later, Bridget began having flashbacks where she relived the moment the boy was hit. This happened repeatedly and 'out of the blue', as she put it, and each time the episode left her exhausted and tearful, unable to resume whatever she'd been doing for at least half an hour. She was also plagued by the thought that she could have done more, despite repeated reassurances from the ambulance crew.

Bridget received EMDR (Eye Movement Desensitisation and Reprocessing), a treatment recommended for PTSD, and her flashbacks and negative ruminations stopped. However, she was left feeling afraid to walk along any street where there might be cyclists, thus making it more or less impossible for her to get out and about. She was then referred to me for help to overcome agoraphobia.

She was highly motivated to overcome her fears and get back to work, and she responded well. During our sessions, however, Bridget began to talk about a problem she'd often battled when she was on the ward – long before witnessing the accident. She explained that she'd frequently feel breathless and panicky, and unable to decide which of the vast number of tasks required of her she should undertake. She agreed to discuss this with her manager, and, meanwhile, she began to set aside ten minutes before each shift for mindfulness practice. When at work, she made sure she spent three minutes of each break in mindful awareness as well. We also worked through Step Four together, focusing in particular on how she could plan her workload more realistically. These changes worked so well for Bridget that she was invited to present her approach to the other nurses on her ward, so that everyone could feel calmer and in better control of their duties.

Bridget's case is an example of someone who had experienced a terrifying situation, an event so distressing that it caused her to become hyper alert, constantly anticipating danger. When that happens, that is when you believe that something terrible is just about to happen *but it has not yet done so,* then rather than fighting or fleeing, you'll begin to feel anxious. The symptoms of anxiety – palpitations, breathlessness, sweating, nausea, an inability to focus on anything except what's worrying you – are entirely the result of having prepared to respond to some sort of threat, but then finding that you're unable to release yourself from that state of preparation. When there's nothing actually there that you can react to, you'll start to feel blocked, tense and frightened.

I hope this helps you understand why, if you suffer from chronic anxiety, it's so incredibly important that you become mindful. When you learn to relax sufficiently and observe yourself and your surroundings, you'll start to recognise the conditions that cause you to feel highly anxious. That awareness will allow you to distinguish between any real dangers and those that are merely imagined or exaggerated. Once you're able to understand and accept that there's no need to remain in such a heightened state of arousal, you'll want to find ways to regain focus on your everyday activities. That's what mindfulness practice will allow you to do. That awareness will, in turn, allow you to distinguish between real dangers and those that are merely imagined or exaggerated.

In summary, know that you can trust yourself to recognise when a danger is real. You can trust yourself, too, to deal with it immediately and as effectively as you know how. If, on the other hand, the danger is imagined or exaggerated, then once you've learned to become more mindful you'll be able to put your worry into perspective and prevent the crippling discomfort that results from chronic anxiety.

There's no need for 'preparation'

You may wonder whether it will be necessary to take a mindfulness training course in order to learn this new way of being. This won't be necessary because what I'm teaching you is not what you'd learn if you take on formal mindfulness training. What I'm offering is not a 'programme', and you don't need to set aside practice sessions. I'm introducing you to a new way of *being*, rather than asking more *doing* of you.

That's not, however, to say that mindfulness training isn't valuable. It is. A course in mindfulness will offer you the chance to learn a great deal, and it may be something you decide to do once you're living the five steps and feeling eager to learn new things.

Nor do you need to be taught how to meditate. Meditation and mindfulness are two different activities, even though the words are often used interchangeably. They are closely related, it's true. It's also true that you can't meditate without being mindful – although you can be mindful even when you're not formally meditating.

Mindfulness and meditation are alike in one important way – they both require non-judgmental awareness. However, during mindfulness you're aware of what's happening both within you as well as around you, whereas during meditation your focus is inwards and your aim is exclusively to observe your thoughts. Andy Puddicombe, in his book *Get Some Headspace*, describes the difference between meditation and mindfulness delightfully:

'The distinction between meditation and mindfulness may not sound that important, and often the words are used interchangeably. But unless you're about to pack your bags and start life afresh as a monk or a nun, this distinction matters a lot. Because so long as you're living life outside of a mountain retreat, there'll always be a limited amount of time to sit down and practise meditation in a formal, structured way.' (p. 22)

Mindfulness is more than just heightened awareness. There's more to it than simply paying more attention to what's going on around you. It's true that if you start paying more attention to what's happening in the present moment, you'll certainly start feeling more alive. You'll also be less likely to overlook anything, so you'll make fewer mistakes. But when you practise mindfulness you'll be doing far more than simply making sure you're a bit more aware of where you are and what's going on around you. When you practise mindful awareness you not only observe everything more carefully, you observe everything objectively – that is, without making assumptions about what you notice. This is a great deal more challenging than you might suppose!

Because we so often feel rushed as we go about our daily lives, most of us react to what we see prejudicially. That is, in order to learn what we need to learn as quickly as possible, we make assumptions about what we see based on our past experience in similar situations and on our pre-existing beliefs. Rarely do we take in our surroundings as if it's the first time we've noticed them. One way of looking at this is that most of us see what we expect to see, rather than what's actually there. When you're mindfully aware, you'll see the world more accurately.

Years ago, as a research assistant in a psychology department, I was asked to run an experiment in which subjects were asked to describe a small, everyday object for three minutes. When I gave the item – usually a twig or small stone from the garden – to the subject, their first reaction would be something like this: 'There's *no way* I'll have enough to say about this stick/stone for three whole minutes!' Yet without exception, when I'd call time, the subject would ask for 'just a bit longer' because they'd become so interested in that object and wanted to go on exploring and describing it.

Heightened awareness is, therefore, only the first step in learning to be mindful. You need not only be aware, but be aware *without judging*. You'll begin to see things as they actually are. As a consequence, you'll start to become more interested in your surroundings and will develop what many mindfulness teachers refer to as a 'gentle curiosity' about what's going on within and around you.

A new way of being

It's really important to realise that this first step is all about a new way of *being*, any time and any where. It's not another *doing*, another stress-making pressure on your time. Once you adopt this new way of being, you won't be doing more. Instead, you'll be doing what you do more richly. It will be like turning that kaleidoscope – the same pieces are still there, but the pattern they make now looks more beautiful and integrated.

Even taking just a moment to be mindful will enrich your life. Therefore, whenever you remember – and especially whenever you're feeling overwhelmed and stressed – tell yourself that it's worth pausing to remind yourself that you needn't feel anxious. Stop rushing around, just for a moment, and centre yourself. Observe the current situation carefully, without passing judgment, and only then decide what to do next and how best to do it.

That said, if you practise this way of being only from time to time – and crucially, for less than ten minutes a day – then the benefits will be limited to the periods of time when you're mindfully aware, and perhaps for some of you, up to perhaps half an hour afterwards.

If, on the other hand, you wish to fundamentally change the way you approach stressful situations, if you want to live your life more fully and calmly everyday, and if you want to solve whatever problems you face more efficiently and adaptively, then you need to make mindful awareness your habitual response rather than merely an occasional one. That means that you'll need to practise this way of being regularly and often. You will, in essence, need to create a new habit.

To establish this new habit, you'll need to override the one that's already in place – that is, rushing through your day without noticing and *knowing* your life. You'll need to practise the new way until it feels 'automatic'. At that point, you'll no longer have to remind yourself not to panic, or react in the old inappropriate ways, when you feel threatened. In my experience, that means you'll need to practise the new behaviour regularly and often for at least six weeks before it's had a chance to replace non-awareness.

Of course, there will be days when you feel like all you want to do is rush ahead with everything as quickly as possible, rather than making sure you centre yourself and really observe. Try to fight that tendency – it will only rob you of truly living through a time that you'll never have again. Remember that any new behaviour takes effort at first. It's going to take some getting used to, because it's so different from the way most of us attend to what's going on. Furthermore, whenever we start to feel stressed, our first reaction is to revert to our old established ways of behaving.

Find some way to remind yourself regularly that there's a far better way to live your life than simply repeating your old bad habits. The most effective way to do that, I've found, is to make sure that twice a day, every day, you devote five minutes to mindful awareness. Five minutes is long enough to allow your mind and body to settle down and relax. It's also enough time to allow you to feel the difference, to realise how much calmer and in control you're going to feel generally when this is your habitual response to stress.

The best times to be mindful when you're starting out

The best time for that all-important first 'session' of the day is just after you wake up. That way, you'll start each day feeling centred and clear-minded. The way most of my clients choose to do this is to set their alarm five minutes earlier than they normally would do each morning. Try it. When the alarms sounds, sit up in bed and allow yourself to become fully aware of yourself and your surroundings during those five minutes. Then begin your usual morning routine.

On the other hand, you might prefer to set your alarm five minutes earlier and simply begin your usual routine straight away. That extra time will allow you to do everything much more slowly, in mindful awareness. As you get out of bed, think how your arms and legs feel as you stand up. Stretch, and really *feel* that stretch. Think about how the toothbrush feels against your teeth and gums, what the toothpaste looks and smells like, and so on.

You needn't worry, by the way, that if you start your day in such a relaxed manner you'll forget to do something important later, or that in some other way you'll be ill-prepared for the tasks that lie ahead. In truth, you'll be *better* prepared than ever because when you're calm and centred you'll be more alert and clear-headed, able to notice anomalies more quickly and come up with more ways to sort things out. In other words, establishing a mindful attitude each morning will not only help you to appreciate the present. It will also put you in the best frame of mind for making sound plans and for dealing wisely with whatever arises later that day.

You can have your second practice whenever you'd like. I suggest that you establish a regular time, because you'll be less likely to forget that second session if you practise at the same time each day. Furthermore, you'll get the most out of it if you choose a time when you're usually on 'autopilot'. So for example, if during your journey home from work you're usually unaware of your surroundings and you spend the time thinking about what you're planning to do that evening or endlessly reliving moments earlier in the day, then decide instead to carry out this journey in mindful awareness. Notice how your body is feeling as you drive, or while you're sitting on the train or tube, or walking home. Take a good look at the other people around you. Listen to the sounds of the evening or the buzz of the crowds. Take in the scents. Feel the cool air on your skin.

Very soon – within three to six weeks, in my experience – you'll be feeling so confident about your new ability and enjoying the results so much that you'll no longer want to limit yourself to a mere ten minutes each day. Soon, you'll want to stop for a moment whenever something changes in your environment, or whenever you begin any new activity, to centre yourself and truly appreciate the change. You'll also begin to realise that when you are mindful, you make fewer mistakes, you say or do things that you regret less often, and you're less likely to overlook anything valuable when you make decisions.

Very soon, mindfulness will become your way of being.

A taster session

One of the nicest aspects of living mindfully is that anyone can live in this richer way. No preparation is necessary. So why not start right now?

Settle yourself comfortably, preferably somewhere you feel safe and at ease – in a favourite chair in your sitting room or in your bedroom, for example.

Turn off any potential interruptions or distractions. It doesn't matter whether you close your eyes or leave them open. Just do whatever feels better to you.

Now simply observe what's around you or, if you've chosen to close your eyes, observe your thoughts and your physical state. Listen, look, taste, smell, touch – use any and all of your senses – but remember, *only notice*! Do not judge or compare or plan. Merely absorb. It's best if you don't even try to describe to yourself anything you experience. Just drink in every detail.

OK, how long did it take before you found yourself thinking about what you need to do next, or what happened earlier today, or what might be going on elsewhere? Only a few seconds, I would imagine. It's so easy to *know* what to do, but so incredibly difficult actually to *do* it!

It will take days, maybe even weeks, before you can remain fully mindful for much more than a few minutes at a time. But you'll find that you want to practise more and more often, and that you'll notice improvements every time you do so.

Dealing with your 'off' days

Everyone has 'off' days. When you oversleep, or for other reasons miss a time you'd hoped to use for mindfulness practice, there's no need to waste precious energy feeling guilty. These occasions won't constitute a 'setback' or a 'failure' unless you choose to see them in that way. Even on those days, there are plenty of things you can do instead to establish your new habit.

Here are three suggestions you can try at any time:

1. *Do an inventory*
Imagine that you need to describe the space you're in to someone who's never seen it and needs to know that place in every detail. So take, for example, the chair you're sitting in. What sort of wood is it made from? If there's a cushion, what colour is it and what sort of material is it made from? How old do you think the chair might be? Does it match the other chairs in the room? – and so on. This is a good exercise in concentration, and it will wake you up to your immediate surroundings.

2. *Describe a common household object*
Choose something you think you know – one of your everyday spoons, a mug you often use, or a coin, for example. Now describe it to yourself in the minutest detail. Identify precisely the colours, detail every crack or stain, judge the weight, and so on. You'll be surprised

to discover how much you *didn't* know about something you use or see often! You may also find that you come to appreciate it more than you did before you scrutinised it so carefully.

3. *Have a backwards day* (You'll need to do this one on a day when you've a fairly free schedule. If you have children, they'll love it!)

   When you wake in the morning, start off by doing whatever you normally do in the evenings before bedtime. Then go into the kitchen and prepare supper, and enjoy it with your family. Next, go about your usual *afternoon* activities insofar as you can. Lunch is next, then any morning activities. Finish the day with breakfast. This exercise will help you realise how many routines you're tied into. As a result, you may decide to make some changes in your schedule.

Mindfulness is a *re*discovery

Although I've encouraged you to *learn* to be more mindful, perhaps it would be more accurate to say that you need to *re*learn this way of being. Observe a young child for a few minutes and you'll understand what I mean. Babies and young children spend almost all of their time in mindful awareness. Notice the way a baby contemplates the world, or how toddlers behave when they're playing. They're totally absorbed in what they're doing, oblivious to what happened yesterday and unconcerned about what may happen tomorrow. They can show you, better than any adult, how to live mindfully.

Sadly, however, as they grow up, most of them will lose touch with this ability to focus fully on their present reality, largely as a consequence of the world we introduce them into as they grow.

Our modern Western world is bombarded at every turn by distractions. Telephones are ringing everywhere we go, emails and texts announce their arrival in our inboxes, billboards loom out at us along every main street, and TV screens blare their offerings continually inside almost every public and even private space. We're overwhelmed with far more information than we could ever take in properly, and a disproportionate amount of it is negative and/or frightening.

The reason for this current state of affairs – both the cascade of distractions and the proliferation of bad news – is entirely commercial. Let's start with the constant distractions. Their main function is to interfere with our ability to concentrate, to ensure that we're less likely to make considered decisions and that instead, we're more open to outside suggestions. When we're continually interrupted by adverts, we're more likely to buy what those adverts offer us. The repetition and the constant intrusions 'scramble' our own train of thought, and make it more likely we'll simply accept what we hear and see around us, without challenging the messages.

Similarly, the bad news we see everywhere also interrupts our thoughts. It puts us on alert and makes us feel uneasy, perhaps even anxious, and keen to find out more. As a result, we continue to pay attention to those sources of information, instead of relaxing and thinking for ourselves.

In this heightened state of arousal it's easy to forget that bad news isn't the only sort of news around. There are also plenty of cheerful stories to tell. But it's only bad news that encourages us to buy more newspapers, turn on our computers and TVs more often, and in any number of other ways allow others to think for us. We've become used to being told what to think about, and we're lazy about turning off those biased sources of information. In truth, we can tone things down and turn things off more often, if only we choose to do so.

Furthermore, the younger we are when we start being bombarded by outside interruptions, the sooner we come to rely on sources outside ourselves to stimulate us, rather than to choose our own amusements and to think more often for ourselves. I'm convinced that's one of the reasons why there's been such an enormous rise recently in the incidences of ADHD (Attention Deficit Hyperactivity Disorder). Children are simply learning to be distractable, rather than to rely on their own inner resources to come up with things to do and to discover ways to solve problems.

Mindfulness vs positive thinking

Adopting a positive mind-set, i.e. focusing only on that which you hope or wish to see, is assumed to be a 'good idea'. In fact, positive thinking is *not* a wise way to live. It does *not* necessarily make us happier or calmer.

Positive thinking is not the same thing as mindfulness. Positive thinking demands selective focus. Books like *The Secret* encourage you to concentrate fully on the good things in life and overlook negativity. I believe that this effort to limit what you perceive is much more effortful than mindful thinking, and it can lead you to conjure up a false view of reality. The mindful approach suggests instead that you become aware of and accept reality as it is, without being selective and without polarising what you perceive into 'positive' and 'negative' categories. When you're mindful, you consider everything to be of equal worth. You don't have to 'screen out' what you deem to be negative or unacceptable.

Positive thinking also encourages you to focus on the future, and to think about what you want to have or to achieve that isn't yours already. This implies that the only thing you can be certain of in your present life is that it is inadequate and unfulfilling, because you don't yet have everything you want. Mindful awareness is different. It allows you to feel fulfilled and satisfied all the time. When you are mindful, you simply appreciate what is yours already.

Some proponents of positive thinking take the matter even further. Some of them go so far as to suggest that diseases and ageing are 'all in the mind' and that if you simply banish thoughts about being ill or growing old, and think only about health and youthfulness instead, then health and eternal youth is what you will have. This is at best unrealistic. At worst, it can cause people who are already suffering to feel helpless and even worse about themselves and their circumstances. This is particularly true of those individuals who – through accident or genetic inheritance – have become ill or have aged prematurely.

Of course, positive thinking does have its place. Primarily, expecting the best outcome can keep your spirits up during tough times. However, when the outcome isn't what you'd hoped – and it won't be every time – you're bound to feel disappointed. If, instead, you hope for the best *but accept with grace whatever happens,* you'll feel calm and avoid unnecessary disappointment.

In my experience, self-acceptance coupled with an appreciation of your surroundings and your own unique abilities – the essence of mindful awareness – is more closely related to happiness and a sense of calm than goal-orientated positive thinking.

Squaring mindfulness with the need to plan and set goals

Another cause of unhappiness that most of us adopt blindly is the belief that the only way to be really successful is to set lofty goals and then focus single-mindedly on trying to achieve them. At first glance, this appears utterly incompatible with mindfulness, and as a result you may be left with the feeling that you can't live mindfully while getting an education, staking out a career, or possibly even raising a family. How can these be achieved without forward planning and goal-setting?

The secret to finding a way to live more mindfully amid the demands of today's world lies in your *motivation* when you set goals and then work hard to meet them.

If your aim is to be admired and to have lots of wealth or other material goals, then you need to fix your mind on what you don't yet have, on how you'll get hold of these things, and how others are reacting to you as you acquire them. This will increase the chances that you'll gain that praise and those possessions. However, you won't feel calm doing so and even if you are happy as a result, that feeling won't last for long. Why?

Firstly, admiration is a fickle sort of regard. It can all too easily turn to envy. So in order to continue to be admired you must remain on your guard about what others are thinking. Furthermore, you'll begin to feel the need to maintain their approval by creating and achieving ever more goals. Secondly, if wealth and possessions are your goals, although they'll please you in the short term, they'll almost certainly breed a desire to have more and ever more. Your wealth will also create work and worry for you, as it says in *The Prophet*:

'For what are your possessions but things you keep and guard for fear you may need them tomorrow?'

If, on the other hand, you set yourself a goal but then you focus fully on *the process of achievement* – that is, on what you're doing and how well you're doing it in the present moment – rather than on what you might get later as a result, or on what others think of you, then you'll feel fulfilled. This process of using your skills and talents fully and immersing yourself in the moment is known as 'flow', and the feeling it gives is nothing short of exhilarating. It also means you perform at your best. Flow, or 'optimal experience', occurs when you choose to stretch yourself to your limits to accomplish something difficult and worthwhile. When you discover (or more likely, rediscover) your passions in Step 3, you'll learn more about this concept.

Mindfulness can also enhance performance. Perhaps the best way to illustrate the impact that mindful awareness can have on performance is to let an Olympic gold medallist explain. Here's what rowing champion Steve Redgrave said in an interview in the *Daily Telegraph*:

> *'If, during an Olympic campaign, you start to think for a second about what you are going to do afterwards, that can detract from what you are doing in the present. You have to channel all your energies into your immediate performance in an Olympic sport, and trust that the rest of life will take care of itself.'*

(13 July 2012, p. 10)

Another Olympic competitor, the swimmer Ellen Gandy, agrees. She recounts the personal cost of losing her focus:

'I vividly remember sitting in the call room before the semi-final of the 200 metres butterfly (in Beijing, 2008). Michael Phelps was in the next race, going for one of his gold medals, and I just became fixated on what it must be like for him to be in that position. I got too easily distracted and was not focused on my own preparation, and my swimming suffered.'

(*Telegraph*, 27 July 2012, p. 14)

Most of us never really stop to observe *how* we do what we do. You'll never get to know how much more capable you could actually be if you limit yourself to specific endpoints or restrictive goals. Mindful awareness gives you the opportunity to reach your full potential more surely than if your efforts are limited by the goals you focus on. Here's an example that illustrates what I mean.

Before 1954, no one believed that a human being could run a mile in less than four minutes. However, on the sixth of May that year, a young British athlete named Roger Bannister finished a one-mile race in 3 minutes and 59.4 seconds.

This was a remarkable feat in itself, but what followed was even more remarkable. Just 46 days later, the Australian runner John Landy broke Bannister's record, and other runners soon followed suit. It appears that those upper limits on speed were all in the mind, and that once the athletes set aside their old expectations and instead focused fully on their performance, they began to run faster than anyone had believed was possible.

Mindfulness and the pressure to multitask

Yet another pressure we face is that we're all encouraged to multitask, the implication being that if you don't you'll be left behind by those who work at several tasks simultaneously. Mindfulness, in contrast, would appear to slow you down.

However, this viewpoint misses the key value of adopting a mindful outlook. When you're mindful you'll feel calmer and more content with your life, and you'll do whatever you choose to do as thoroughly and as well as you possibly can. That means you'll make fewer mistakes. No one suggests that if you practise mindfulness you'll get things done more quickly; but you will be better at what you do, and you'll feel more fulfilled generally. The same cannot be said about merely working as quick as you can.

However, there's a more fundamental flaw in the argument that promotes multitasking. The truth is, when you try to multitask you'll actually complete *each* task more slowly, and you'll make more mistakes than you would if you tackled one task at a time and gave it your full attention.

You don't believe me? Then I suggest you take this little test that I've adapted from Dave Crenshaw's excellent book, *The Myth of Multitasking*:

Is multitasking really the fastest way to get things done?

Get out a piece of paper, a pen or pencil, and ask a friend to time you. Sit down at a table or desk, and copy the following phrase at the top of your paper:

'Multitasking is not as good as you suppose'
You will now do two short timed tests. You may do them in either order.

1. *Multitasking*
   You're going to write out the phrase you just wrote once again. This time, however, you'll also write a series of numbers (1 to 35) at the same time, as follows: rewrite the phrase at the top of the page. However, each time you write a letter, write a number immediately below it. So for example, when you write 'M', underneath you'll write '1'. When you write 'u', underneath you'll write '2', and so on. Work as quickly as you can, and ask your friend to time you. Record your time.

2. *Working sequentially*
   This time, you're going to write out the phrase AND the series of numbers (1 to 35) as follows: rewrite the phrase, and then beneath the phrase write the numbers 1 to 35. Do this as quickly as you can, and ask your friend to time you. Record your time.

   Now, compare the two times. Which instructions allowed you to finish the task more quickly? Under which condition did you make fewer errors?

Unless you are unlike everyone else I've ever tested, you will have taken almost twice as long to complete the task under the multitasking instructions as you took to complete the task when you worked sequentially. You will also have made more mistakes under the multitasking instructions.

This exercise makes it clear that we've all been under an illusion for some time. In truth, the human brain – and computers too, for that matter – are simply not capable of doing two things simultaneously.

When we believe we're doing two or more things at the same time what's actually happening is that we're switching back and forth from one task to another, so rapidly that we're generally unaware that we're doing so. Crenshaw suggests that a more accurate term for what we're doing is that we're *switchtasking* rather than multitasking. The effort of focusing on one task, then repeatedly setting it aside mentally and taking up another task, costs time and mental effort. That constant juggling, however quickly it's done, adds up, as you've just proved for yourself.

Therefore, when you do your work in mindful awareness you'll be more efficient, and you'll make fewer errors because you're fully focused on what you're doing at any given moment. To help you feel even more satisfied about your ability to meet challenges well, in Step Four you will learn how to prioritise what you wish to accomplish, so that whatever matters most to you will always be accomplished first.

Mindfulness is not competitive

There's no such thing as being 'properly' mindful or being 'good enough' at this way of being, because that would involve judging your 'performance'. Remember that being mindful does *not* involve passing judgment! It's about paying attention fully, to yourself and to what's happening around you, in the present moment, and without comparing or judging.

That said, you will notice a change within yourself once you're able to remain mindful for any sustained period of time – that is, for five minutes at least. You'll become aware of a most wonderful sense of calm and wellbeing, and a deep release of tension both in your mind and in your body. At that point, you're unlikely to need reminding to practise this way of living. It will have become self-motivating.

Mindful awareness is also an excellent preparation for whatever comes next in your life. Because this way of being allows you to gather accurate information without prejudging what's going on it means that, when you look at your options and choose how you wish to take action, you're most likely to choose wisely. You'll also do whatever you decide to do as well as you possibly can. This is yet another reason why there's no need to think about 'improvements' or 'getting better'. Everything you do will be done as well as you could have done at the time.

How much mindfulness is enough?

The most calm and fulfilling way to live your life is to be fully mindful at all times. However, in today's noisy world, it's also one of the most difficult ways of being.

Therefore, the best way to live is to do so in mindful awareness as often as you can. You can never 'overdo' it! At the same time, however, be patient with yourself when/if you slip back into the old habits of inattention and distraction. As soon as you become aware that this has happened simply refocus on the present moment, on what's happening in and around you, and on what you're doing right now.

The Buddhist monk Thich Nhat Hanh puts it beautifully when he extols the virtues of mindfulness. In his book, *The Miracle of Mindfulness,* he writes:

'Be mindful 24 hours a day, not just during the one hour you may allot for formal meditation or reading scripture and reciting prayers. Each act must be carried out in mindfulness. Each act is a rite, a ceremony. Raising your cup of tea to your mouth is a rite. Does the word "rite" seem too solemn? I use that word in order to jolt you into the realization of the life-and-death matter of awareness.'

(*The Miracle of Mindfulness,* p. 24)

Can mindfulness offer even more than a sense of focus and serenity?

As if these qualities weren't already enough, recent research suggests that you may enjoy another benefit as well – that of keeping your brain as 'young' as possible throughout your life.

The search for 'superagers'

As we grow older, there's general acceptance that our memory – and indeed our brain mass – will gradually decline. However, scientist Theresa Harrison and her team at Northwestern University in Chicago had heard anecdotal reports of individuals who appear to be immune to age-related memory impairment. They therefore decided to seek them out and study them.

'Superagers', as Harrison called them, were defined as individuals over the age of 80 who had episodic memory performance that was at least as good as the average 50 to 65-year-old. They found 12 such people, matched them with 10 elderly and 14 middle-aged 'controls' – that is, individuals whose ability to remember was what was expected for their chronological age – and put all of them through a series of cognitive and memory tests. They were also asked about health and lifestyle issues, for example their education, their diet, the amount of exercise they generally took, and so on. Finally, each subject also agreed to undergo an MRI scan so that the researchers could have a look at the volume and structure of their brains.

Initially, the results seemed perplexing. The 'superagers' weren't exceptionally well educated – in fact, only four of the 12 had even obtained a college degree. None was known to have had unusually superior memory abilities when they were younger. Some exercised five times a week, others not at all. Some had smoked a pack of cigarettes a day for over 20 years while others had never smoked at all. Some drank alcohol every day while others were teetotal.

Some had lived apparently relatively stress-free lives, while others had lost partners or in other ways lived through a distressing experience. One had survived the Holocaust.

It was only when the team looked at the results of the MRI scans that a consistent picture began to emerge. 'Superagers' appear to have a significantly thicker cortex – the part of the brain responsible for attention and awareness, as well as memory and language – than others of their chronological age. In fact, a 'superagers' cortex looked more like that of the controls who were nearly 30 years younger than themselves!

It is important to note that these findings are in the very early stages of analysis and that the study was only published in the autumn of 2012. We do not yet know whether the brains of these 'superagers' were different from birth. However, there's no reason to despair. We need not accept that our brains will decline as we age. There are strong indications that we can do a lot to maintain – even enhance – brain function, and one of the best ways is to be mindful as often as possible.

The pleasure of seeing the world in fresh ways

Careful observation is a delight because when you observe with care and without making a preconceived judgment, you may suddenly see something new, or see what you've always known was there in new ways. Pat Wolseley, a renowned botanist, described how much participants were enjoying a recent nationwide initiative, the Open Air Laboratories Project, or OPAL. The aim of this project is to make us all more aware of the natural world and our impact on it.

Professor Wolseley described the ability she teaches to those who join the project, to observe what we normally see with greater care – as she puts it, 'to be given a third eye'. One of her students, seeing as if for the first time a tiny lichen growing on a plant, exclaimed that suddenly what she was observing became 'like eyelashes growing on a branch'.

This is what careful, fresh observation can do. Such delicate beauty is all around, if only we will take the time to observe carefully.

How to Live More Mindfully

1. Start becoming more mindful today. Allow yourself, as often as possible, the opportunity to make every moment one in which you're fully alive.

2. Become aware of all of your senses – of sound, touch, scent, taste and vision – rather than just relying on the last of these.

3. Give yourself the best start possible each day. Spend the first five minutes of every morning in mindful awareness. Wake five minutes earlier than you would do normally, and use those five minutes either to immerse yourself fully in the moment, experiencing the world just as it is right now. Or you can start your morning routine

---

as usual, but do everything more slowly, in mindful awareness.

4. Choose a second five-minute period later in the day for another session of mindful awareness. Encourage yourself to become fully aware of what's going on both within you and around you. At the same time, try not to criticise, evaluate, or make judgments. Simply stay in the present moment and remain gently curious. When your mind wanders to the past or speculates on the future, bring yourself back to the present moment. The best times to choose for this second practice are when you're doing something you've done repeatedly for some time, those occasions when you tend to go onto 'automatic pilot'.

5. Practise mindfulness for at least one minute during every meal. Enjoy the colours, scents, textures and tastes of what you're eating.

6. Whenever you're moving, try to do so in mindful awareness. Feel your muscles as they stretch and contract. Notice how you're breathing.

7. Whenever you start a new activity, begin whatever you do by grounding yourself first in mindful awareness – that is, by taking account fully of what's going on at that moment both within and around you, without

comparing or judging what you're experiencing. Simply observe.

8. End every day in mindful awareness. As you lie in bed, feel the warmth spreading through your body as you relax. Notice your breathing as it slows and deepens, and your body as it sinks into your mattress.

9. Remember that even a minute spent in mindful aware-ness is a minute lived fully. Make every moment count.

FINALLY, A TALE

I'd like to close this chapter by paraphrasing a short story by Leo Tolstoy that was first published in 1903. The original text can be found in *Twenty Three Tales*. Tolstoy called it simply 'Three Questions', and it illustrates elegantly the benefits of living life mindfully:

There was once a King who decided that, if he knew the answer to three questions, he would never fail in anything he might choose to do.

He therefore had it proclaimed throughout his kingdom that he would give a rich reward to anyone who could answer the following three questions:

What is the right time to do each thing?

Who are the most important people to listen to?
What is the most important thing to do at all times?

Many learned men journeyed to the King's palace and gave their answer. In reply to the first question there were those who advised him to draw up a strict schedule and live strictly according to it. Others suggested he appoint a council of wise men to advise him; still others proposed that he consult a magician.

To the second question some said the people he most needed to listen to were doctors. Others suggested priests; still others told him that the most important people to listen to were the warriors.

The answers to the third question were equally varied. Some said that the most important thing in the world was science. Others argued that it was religion, and so it went on. There was no agreement.

The King wasn't happy with any of the answers, so he gave no one the reward. However, he now wanted even more to know the answers to his three questions. He'd heard of a hermit who was widely renowned for his wisdom, and he determined to ask this wise man for some answers.

The hermit lived in a wood that he refused to leave. Furthermore, he made a point to see only the poor and humble, and not anyone of wealth or power. So the King put on poor man's clothing and ordered his bodyguards to remain some distance from the hermit's hut so he could journey there alone.

When he reached the hermit's home he found the old man digging the ground in his garden. He nodded to the King, but then went on with his labour. It was obviously hard work for him, for he was breathing heavily.

The King approached the old man and said, 'I have come to ask you three questions. What is the right time to do each thing? Who are the people I need to attend to most? And what is the most important thing to do at all times?'

The hermit appeared to listen, but he did not answer. Instead, he continued digging the earth. After a while, the King said, 'You appear to be tired. Let me help you.' The old man thanked him and handed him the spade.

The King began to dig the rows the hermit had begun. As he worked, he repeated his questions. Still the hermit did not answer. The King dug more rows, and again he asked the questions. Still the hermit was silent. At last the King put down the spade and said, 'I came to you for an answer to my questions. If you will not answer me, then I will go home.'

The hermit's reply was unexpected. 'Do you hear someone running?' he asked. 'Let us see who it might be.'

The King looked around, and he saw a man running out from the woods. The man held his hands against a wound in his stomach from which the blood flowed freely. As he reached the King, he fell to the ground in a faint.

The King and the hermit opened the man's shirt to reveal a large knife wound to his stomach. They cleaned the wound, and the King used his own shirt to staunch the bleeding, rinsing the cloth repeatedly until at last the bleeding stopped. At that point the man revived and asked for a drink. The King fetched some fresh water from the stream and gave it to him.

By this time, the sun had set and it had begun to cool down. Together the King and the hermit carried the wounded man into the hut and laid him down on the bed, where he promptly fell asleep. The King, tired from the exertions of the day, crouched on the threshold and he, too, fell asleep.

When he awoke in the morning light, the King was surprised to see the wounded man bent over him, gazing at him with shining eyes. 'Please forgive me!' the man cried.

'What is there to forgive?' asked the King. 'I do not even know you.'

'Ah, but I know you,' replied the man. 'You killed my brother and you seized all his property, and I swore revenge upon you. I heard that you were going alone to speak to the hermit, so I decided to lie in wait and ambush you as you returned from your visit.'

'When much time had passed and you did not return, I left my hiding place to seek you. However, your bodyguards spotted me. They recognised me and tried to kill me. I managed to escape, but I would have bled to death had you and the old man here not tended my wounds, given me water and offered me shelter.'

'I came to kill you, and now you have saved my life. Now if I live, I wish to serve you and bid my sons to do the same. Will you forgive me?'

The King was moved by the man's gratitude, and he was glad to have made peace with an enemy. Therefore, not only did he forgive the man, but he sent his personal physician to attend to him. He also promised to restore the man's family property.

After the King had made his peace and taken leave of the man, he turned again to the hermit and once more he asked him to answer the three questions. The hermit looked at him in surprise and replied, 'Why do you ask me again? Your questions have been answered already!'

'I do not understand,' said the King. 'Tell me how this can be.'

The hermit explained: 'Yesterday when you met me, had you not pitied my weakness and stayed to help me dig my garden, rather than returning straight away to your bodyguards, that man would have attacked you. You would have regretted not helping me. Therefore, the most important time was when you helped me dig. I was the most important person to you, and helping me was your most important objective at that moment. Then later when the wounded man came into our midst, the most important time was when you were tending his wounds. If you had not helped him, he would have died without making his peace with you. So at that moment, he was the most important person, and helping him was your most important task.'

The wise men went on. 'Always remember this: there is only one time that is important, and that is right now. Right now is the only time when we can know for certain that we will be able to make a difference.'

'The most important person in your life is whoever you are with right now, because you cannot know with certainty whether you will be given the opportunity to be with that person again, or to be with anyone else, in future.'

'And finally, the most important task to undertake is to try to make life richer and better for the person you are currently with, for that is the purpose in life for all of us.'

You can know with certainty only this.

You have this moment, wherever you are and with whomever is there with you.

Mindfulness will allow you to make the most of every moment of your life and therefore to live the richest and best life possible. When you are mindful, you will know what it is to feel truly calm and fulfilled.

Now that you've created the foundation that is *The Key to Calm*, it's time for a maintenance check. Step Two will show you how best to care for your mind and body, focusing on four key areas: Breathing, Movement, Rest and Nutrition.

Step Two:
Take Care of Your Best Asset

'*. . . And your body is the harp of your soul,*
And it is yours to bring forth sweet music from it or
confused sounds.'

The Prophet, Kahlil Gibran

During the course of your life you will almost certainly move house more than once. You'll travel. You'll stay with friends. You will, over time, have inhabited many places.

However, there's one place you'll always inhabit, one place that will always be with you, and that is your body. The health of your body dictates how easily you can move about, how much you can do, and how quickly and clearly you can think. In short, the health of your body determines how likely it is that you'll accomplish what you want to accomplish in life.

And yet, most of the time we don't bother to pay much attention to how well we're feeling, or to make sure we keep ourselves in top condition. In fact, many people are likely to spend more time trying to alter the shape of their body or to change a particular feature than they are to looking after their health and wellbeing.

When things go wrong, however, suddenly it's a different story. When we fall ill or suffer an injury, we're often caught off-guard. Why did something go wrong? Why should this happen to me, and why now? A good friend of mine, a GP, tells me that many of the patients who come to see her appear perplexed when they recount their symptoms, at a loss about why they should have a problem. She'll point out gently that, given what a marvellously complex system we inhabit, we shouldn't be surprised when something goes wrong. Instead, we should be amazed that most of the time, everything works as well as it does!

In this step I'll be offering you the most-up-to date information about your health and psychological well-being, so you'll know how to take the best possible care of your mind and body. The effort, you'll discover, will be more than worthwhile, because when you're as physically healthy and as psychologically balanced as possible, a sense of peace and serenity will inevitably follow.

There are four cornerstones of good health. These are Breathing, Movement, Rest and Nutrition. Let's start with the most fundamental of all . . .

BREATHING

You may wonder why I'm devoting an entire section to breathing. Isn't this something we just 'do'?

If you've ever taken a yoga or Pilates class, if you've learned to swim, or if you've ever tried to meditate, you will know that the way we breathe is fundamental to how well we perform and think. Learning to breathe adaptively is absolutely critical to achieving a sense of calm and wellbeing, to performing at your best, and to feeling in control of your life. Nonetheless, it may seem surprising that anyone would need to 'learn' to do something that is, after all, so automatic. We'll breathe whether we think about doing so or not. However, because of today's stressful, sedentary lifestyle, many of us have developed poor breathing habits. We breathe as if we're constantly preparing to deal with some major threat, but then – unlike when we lived simpler and less technological lives – we find ourselves unable to defuse that threat. As a result, we remain 'poised for battle' for long periods of time, without the opportunity to take any action. This leads to a build-up of oxygen in the body. When we don't release excess oxygen by dealing with the threat, the prolonged imbalance of gases in the body creates a number of unpleasant symptoms including palpitations, sweating, nausea and confusion. These symptoms in turn increase our stress levels and make us feel even more threatened.

If, therefore, you're someone who spends much of the day sitting down, and if you often feel stressed and helpless, then you almost certainly need to learn to breathe more adaptively. Don't, however, fall into the trap of thinking that if you simply breathe more deeply, that will sort you out. That will actually make matters worse! Here's why.

When you feel threatened, your natural reaction is to prepare to deal with the threat, by fighting it or by running away from it. Either way, your body requires plenty of oxygen.

Therefore, when you're chronically stressed you've *already* been breathing in more oxygen than necessary for some time. Some of us do so by breathing more shallowly but more rapidly than usual, and some do so by breathing more and more deeply, that is 'grabbing' for breath. Either way, effortful deep breathing will only make things worse, not better.

There's a far more helpful and effective way to breathe yourself calm, and the best way to understand how to do it is to think about two aspects of adaptive breathing. The first is balance – creating an optimal balance of gases in your body – and the second is control – feeling that you can control how quickly you breathe, and learning to breathe as slowly as is comfortably possible. Let's consider each aspect separately.

Balance

When you're under pressure your first reaction is to inhale deeply and/or rapidly, to draw oxygen into the bloodstream to fuel your muscles and to prepare your lungs for exertion. That's fine if you really do respond physically, because the excess oxygen you will have taken in will be used well, as you run or attack.

However, if you must remain stationary – for example, if you're sitting in your car in a traffic jam, if you're being criticised in a meeting, or if you're stuck in front of a frozen computer screen – that excess oxygen will start to cause uncomfortable physical symptoms such as tingling, palpitations or nausea. Those symptoms will in turn make you feel even *more* threatened, and therefore likely to breathe in even *more* oxygen. Thus a vicious circle is established. Many of you will recognise the long-term results of feeling chronically exhausted, vaguely nauseous and unable to concentrate.

Therefore, the first thing you need to do is to get rid of that extra oxygen and re-establish equilibrium within your body. You can do this most readily if you remember always to breathe in through your nose (we take in less oxygen through the nose than we do through the mouth). It matters less how you exhale. You may do so either through your nose or through your mouth, although if you're feeling particularly breathless (paradoxically, that usually means you're in oxygen *excess*), exhaling through your mouth will help you feel balanced and calmer more quickly. It's also important that your in-breath and your out-breath are of more or less equal length. Try counting to yourself, 1001, 1002, 1003 as you breathe in, and then do the same in reverse – 1003, 1002, 1001 – as you breathe out.

You'll need to breathe in this slower, more controlled way for three to five minutes before you'll notice a significant improvement in the way you're feeling. If you're breathing at the rate of about ten breaths a minute (that's inhaling while counting to 1003, and then exhaling while counting from 1003), then 30 to 40 of these 'counting' breaths will be about right. If you prefer, you can count to 1004, or even to 1005 as you breathe. Of course, the slower you breathe, the fewer breaths you'll need to take before you obtain a sense of calm. Just remember to breathe out at the same speed you breathe in.

Control

By breathing in this steady slower manner and by counting your breaths, you automatically establish some control over the most basic of your physical functions. You'll find that this simple exercise has profound and comforting side effects.

When you start to feel in control of your breathing, you'll also begin to feel more in control of your life. Furthermore, as you rebalance your body's chemistry you'll find that you're able to think more clearly and logically. Not only will that feel reassuring in itself, but you'll also be better able to sort out any problems you may be facing.

You can practise this way of breathing any time and any where. In fact, the more often you practise, the sooner it will become an established habit – or perhaps I should say it will become *re*-established as a habit, because that's the way we naturally breathe when we're calm and relaxed. Watch a contented baby or a young child breathing and you'll realise that you've merely lost touch with a healthy natural pattern.

When you breathe in this manner, the most important thing to remember is to breathe evenly, to make sure that each in-breath takes about the same amount of time as each out-breath. Don't worry about how fast or slow you're breathing overall, nor about how many breaths you're taking each minute. You'll feel calm sooner if you simply concentrate on establishing an even rate of breathing.

In summary, then: when you're feeling tense, the fastest

way to calm down is through the breath. Start by centring yourself. Focus inward and think about your body. In particular, check that your neck and shoulders are as relaxed as possible. Now, begin breathing in through your nose, then breathing out through your mouth, as evenly and as slowly as feels comfortable. I've suggested you establish an even rate by counting 1001, 1002, 1003. However, if counting to 1004, or even 1005, feels better for you, that's fine. Just match the length of each in-breath to that of its corresponding out-breath.

The speed that feels most comfortable for most adults is, by the way, an indication of physical condition and state of mind. If you feel comfortable breathing slowly, you're probably already in good physical condition. It also means you've begun to calm down.

You'll find that you'll feel particularly well if you breathe in this manner during the two five-minute periods when you practise mindfulness each day. Your ultimate aim is, of course, to breathe this way all the time.

How to Breathe For Calm

Although we think of breathing as an innate and totally automatic process, the way we breathe is learned. If you often feel stressed and are not as fit as you'd like to be, you probably breathe shallowly and unevenly. The symptoms this sort of breathing produces will increase your sense of threat and anxiety.

The secret to adaptive breathing is to breathe slowly and evenly, in through your nose and out through your mouth. This increases your sense of control – not only over your breathing, but also over your life generally – and will rebalance your body chemistry so you can think most clearly and logically.

In order to notice a significant improvement in the way you're feeling, you need to breathe adaptively for between three and five minutes. This is easily achieved by taking 30 to 40 breaths.

You can use this technique any time, any where; whenever you feel stressed and/or unable to think clearly. It's particularly beneficial to use adaptive breathing during your two mindful awareness sessions each day.

MOVEMENT

Human beings are designed to move. Our muscles are healthiest, our mood is sunniest, and our minds are clearest when we can move about freely.

That means that today's lifestyle with its emphasis on screen-based, sedentary ways has done us no favours. Most of us are less toned than we're designed to be. We breathe too shallowly. It's now common for far too many of us to suffer chronic aches and pains.

But you can change all that, simply by prioritising

movement. If you make it a priority to keep yourself in good physical condition, not only will you be healthier and suffer fewer aches and pains, you'll also think more clearly and feel more positive, calm and self-confident.

The knock-on effects of being in good physical condition

There are a number of ways that physical fitness helps to create a sense of calm and wellbeing. First, when you focus fully on how your body feels and how deeply and slowly you're breathing you are, in effect, practising mindfulness.

A second benefit is increased self-confidence. If you know you're in good physical condition, you'll feel more confident about getting out and mixing with other people. That in turn means you'll have more opportunities to do the things you want to do, so you'll feel happier and more fulfilled.

You're also more likely to be popular with others. That's because, when you feel good about yourself, you won't be anxiously focusing on what others may think about you, so you'll be able to take a genuine interest in the people you're with. Research has shown that when we appear interested in others, they're more likely to consider us to be attractive and likeable.

When you move about regularly – and particularly when you work out aerobically – your body chemistry will be more balanced. As you breathe more deeply the increased oxygen you're taking in is carried to your muscles, so you'll feel stronger. As more oxygen reaches your brain you'll think more clearly. After about ten minutes of steady movement your body will begin to produce endorphins. These chemicals promote a sense of wellbeing. Furthermore, the output of cortisol, the alerting chemical, stops spiking and steadies out at a lower level as you exercise so although you feel alert, that feeling isn't tainted with anxiety.

After about 30 minutes of steady movement, the level of endorphins you'll be producing will inhibit your ability to feel pain. At this point, many people say they feel euphoric – whether that's a result of pain suppression, or a direct function of the endorphin levels is not clear.

Aerobic exercise also increases the level of two more brain chemicals, serotonin and norepinephrine. These are the 'feel good' neurotransmitters. The effect is so consistently positive that some studies have suggested that regular aerobic exercise can be as beneficial as antidepressant medication when it comes to preventing a recurrence of depression.

Finally, if you make good physical health a top priority you'll stay stronger and more flexible and, as a result, you'll be less likely to suffer from chronic aches and pains. That in turn means you'll be less tired – few things are more tiring than chronic pain – and thus find it easier to focus on what's good about your life right now, rather than what's distressing you.

The four foundation stones on which to build fitness

There are four aspects to consider when you incorporate more movement into your life: strength, endurance, flexibility, and clarity of mind. Taken together, these help you stay in the best shape possible for you.

Let's look at each of these in turn:

Strength: Can you lift, hold and carry what's required of you in the course of a normal day? Can you move from one place to another without your legs feeling overly tired or weak? Can you bend down and stand back up with relative ease?

Endurance: Are you able to complete your normal physical tasks without becoming exhausted? Can you cover reasonable distances without feeling totally out of breath?

Flexibility: Can you bend, turn and stretch in the ways you need to, to accomplish tasks necessary to your daily living without experiencing undue discomfort?

Clarity of mind: Are you able easily to centre yourself and remain focused when you wish to be? Is your memory as good as you want it to be? Are you generally as upbeat and optimistic as you'd like to be?

Exercises That Create a Healthy Body

Taking into account the four aspects of movement, the two exercises that incorporate all four most comprehensively are swimming and dancing. Gardening comes a close second; the only aspect it may not address as well as do swimming and dancing is endurance. Running, jogging and cycling are great for endurance and for strengthening certain areas of your body, but they don't necessarily help you develop flexibility. Yoga, martial arts and Pilates are brilliant ways to encourage flexibility and focus, and Pilates in particular strengthens core muscles.

Walking is the most convenient form of exercise, because you don't need any special equipment. Furthermore, very little preparation is involved, and it's probably the easiest form of exercise to integrate into your existing schedule. Housework is no doubt the most useful – but at the same time, probably the least interesting or enjoyable!

Any workout that allows you to become aerobic – that is, to breathe steadily and deeply as a result of steady movement – will enhance your state of mind, because you'll release endorphins, the 'feel-good' hormone.

Above all, however, the best exercises are the ones you're most likely to keep doing, even on days when you don't feel motivated.

There's no need to 'go for the burn'

It's not necessary to work out vigorously to achieve big gains through movement. For our purposes, moving steadily for a period of time is the key. This is far more important than how hard you push yourself. If you do wish to move vigorously, take advice from your doctor about what constitutes safe and healthy exercise for you and remember always to warm up properly first.

Getting started

The first and most important thing to do is to see your doctor, and discuss with them the activities that will be safe for you to develop, and how hard they advise you to work at them. You might then meet with a personal trainer or fitness instructor who can help you design a programme that fits in well with the rest of your schedule. Better yet – and cheaper – however, is to try the following mental exercise. Think back to when you were between nine and twelve years old. What did you most enjoy doing during that time in your life? Did you prefer being indoors or outdoors? Did you seek out the company of others, for example to play team sports, or were you happier when you were engaged in solo activities? Did you most enjoy sports that required short bursts of energy – diving into the swimming pool or sprinting, for example? Or did you more often choose activities that required you to keep moving for longer periods – playing tennis or hiking with friends? See if you can adapt some of these childhood pastimes so they can help you increase your fitness levels now.

The reason why it's so helpful to think back to this age is that it's just before you hit puberty, a time when we're intensely socially aware. Before then, what you choose to do is more likely to reflect your own needs and desires as opposed to your need to 'fit in' with your peers.

Therefore, you're more likely to enjoy a sport if it reflects the interests you had when you were about ten years old. You'll learn more about why this is so in Step Three.

Variety or routine?

If you've found a routine or a specific type of exercise that you love doing, there's nothing wrong at all with repeating it often – if, that is, you do so mindfully. When you move in mindful awareness, no two routines will ever be the same, no matter how alike they appear outwardly. That's because when you focus fully on what you're doing and how you're performing, your vigilance will ensure that you don't 'get in a rut' and, in particular, that you don't develop and repeat bad habits. What you actually choose to do is far less important than always trying to move in the most graceful, balanced way possible, and that you focus fully on what you're doing and how you're doing it.

Distraction or focus?

Some individuals insist that they can only exercise if they do so while listening to music or watching TV. If you feel that the only way you can motivate yourself to take exercise is to distract yourself while doing your workout, then you should consider whether the particular exercise routine you've chosen is the right one for you. Instead of doing things that keep you from thinking about your workout, why not engage the services of a physiotherapist or personal trainer who can help you develop a programme that's so interesting, varied and challenging that you'll *want* to focus on it? Or take up a sport that you've always loved – that way, you'll naturally wish to pay attention to what you're doing.

There's another good reason not to deliberately distract yourself from what you're doing when you're working out. Research has shown that you'll be less efficient – and you'll burn fewer calories – if you distract yourself when exercising. You're also more likely to develop bad habits, habits that mean your posture suffers or that you're more likely to experience chronic aches and pains, if you don't pay attention fully to the way you're moving.

It's definitely the case that when top athletes practise, they don't focus on *anything* except the way they're moving! This laser-beam focus allows them to move as efficiently and powerfully as possible.

It is, however, important to point out that under certain conditions, you can enhance your performance by listening to music when you're exercising. If the activity you've chosen is based on rhythm – for example, you're attending Zumba™ classes or you're learning to dance – then music will help pace your workout, and in those circumstances it can be highly beneficial.

Exercise and chronic pain

Pain management is a difficult clinical problem and, as yet, there's no overall agreement about how best to manage it. Most professionals agree, however, that carefully chosen exercises can help individuals cope. Sufferers rate their pain as less severe, and tolerate it better, if they keep themselves as active as is safely possible.

Whatever the reason, you're right to try to find ways to motivate yourself to work out. Remember, however, that you will need expert guidance to help you choose movements that are safe for you.

First, however, it will help you understand your own feelings better if you know a bit about human reaction to pain.

Our normal reaction when we feel pain is to recoil, to stop what we're doing or move away from whatever's causing the pain. That's a good idea when the source of the pain lies outside the self. However, when we feel pain but there's no ostensible reason for that pain, a different – and really surprising – approach is best. Rather than fighting chronic unexplained pain, the best way to manage it is to pay careful attention to it. Familiarise yourself with how the pain feels and permit that feeling to exist, just as it is.

Unexplained pain seems less intense and more bearable when it's accepted rather than 'fought against'.

Jon Kabat-Zinn, Professor of Medicine Emeritus and probably the best teacher of mindfulness, used this understanding to develop an incredibly effective programme for patients in a Boston hospital who were suffering from pain that couldn't be eliminated, or sometimes not even alleviated. He realised that when sufferers relaxed and 'accepted' the pain, it was easier for them to bear their feelings.

The best way, therefore, to deal with chronic pain is to try to work 'with' it – that is, to recognise it's with you and to respect it as a guide to help you know how hard and how intensively to work out. Your first step will be to see your doctor and discuss with them what you're proposing to do. They'll help you work out safe limits. Then you can devise a programme of movement. You may find this easier if you work with a physiotherapist or sports therapist, one who's experienced in the field of pain management.

Finally, because you may feel less rewarded when you work out than those who don't have to do so in discomfort, make sure you reward yourself after each session with something you do enjoy – a favourite film, a long hot shower, or a favourite healthy food, for example. Knowing a reward is part of the process will also make the pain more bearable while you're exercising.

One of the best examples of how to deal healthily with chronic pain is my client Lynn. Lynn was referred to me to help her find ways to minimise the chance that she'd suffer further episodes of depression – during the past five years, she'd had three courses of antidepressants, each time for six months. Lynn found the side effects of the medication particularly unpleasant and she was keen to find a drug-free alternative to help improve her mood.

When she was in her 20s, Lynn had been a long-distance runner. She'd run a number of marathons and had enjoyed the training enormously. During a particularly gruelling run, however, she'd fallen and twisted her knee. As a result she was advised to give up her sport. About six months later she had her first depressive episode.

Although she learned to use mindful awareness to accept her pain, Lynn still felt that she needed something more to lift her mood. I suggested she meet with a physiotherapist to see if there was any way she could exercise without causing further damage to her knee. The physiotherapist suggested that she take up swimming, which is a good aerobic exercise that is less stressful on joints than is running. Lynn had never learned to swim, but she took to the water with great determination. She now swims several times a week, and to date she has not suffered a relapse of depression for more than ten years.

Exercise and mental wellbeing

1. *Improving memory function*
   There's a good deal of evidence that you can improve your memory if you take regular aerobic exercise. That means moving steadily, enough to raise your heart rate and cause you to breathe more deeply, three or more times a week for at least 20 minutes each session. These

workouts will increase blood flow to the brain and that in turn will make it easier for you to remember things and to think more clearly during and just after your workout. Of course, if the cause of your memory problem is organic – that is, if you suffer from a brain disease or have had a head injury – then exercise can't take away the original cause of your problem. But research suggests that not only will you feel better and think more clearly after exercise, your workouts will also help you stay as fit and healthy as possible. Thus you'll have the best chance of slowing the course of any disease, and recovering from any trauma.

2. *Easing depression and preventing relapse*
Regular aerobic exercise can also alleviate feelings of depression. Regular steady movement releases endorphins and serotonin and depresses cortisol: this will leave you feeling happier and less stressed. Any aerobic exercise will do, although walking and gardening have been studied most often. Furthermore, if exercise is part of an overall treatment programme that includes antidepressant medication, psychotherapy or mindfulness training, the chances that you'll relapse and become depressed again will be reduced significantly.

Finding time for exercise

Knowing the benefits that regular exercise can offer is one thing. Finding the time to gain those benefits may be quite another. In fact, you may even wonder if trying to fit in time to work out will only make you feel more stressed than ever, rather than calmer!

You needn't, however, carve out 'extra' time to exercise. The secret is to start looking out for and taking advantage of opportunities you've probably overlooked, chances to stretch and strengthen your body during the course of your everyday activities. You don't need to set aside an hour for a gym workout unless you wish to do so!

More movement can easily be incorporated into daily life – for example, get off the train or bus sooner than you would normally do and walk the extra distance, climb the stairs instead of taking the lift, or do a bit of house cleaning or gardening instead of watching TV.

Remember, we're not talking here about 'fitness' in the sense of preparing for some sporting event or meeting some workout target. What we're talking about is best health, keeping the body in optimum condition and being able to do whatever you need and wish to do throughout the course of your normal day, with the feeling that you always have a bit 'left over' if ever you need it. There's no need to take 'time out' of your daily schedule to achieve this.

Try, for example, to turn the occasions when you're putting away the shopping into a flexibility workout by exaggerating the stretching and lifting required. When you're stuck with the task of vacuuming, turn that time into a strength and endurance workout. Plan to park at least 15 minutes' walk from your ultimate destination and you'll clarify your mind and feel ready to concentrate on whatever task you're planning to carry out when you arrive.

Probably the most important way to ensure best health through movement is simply to walk whenever and wherever you can. A good way to increase your motivation to walk more is to buy a pedometer and see if you can manage 10,000 steps or more each day. When you're walking, practise improving your ability to focus by concentrating fully on your body, thinking about how your muscles work together so beautifully and automatically as you move. Lift your head high and breathe deeply and evenly. If you have a problem that needs solving or you've forgotten something you wish to recall, bring these questions to mind after you've been walking steadily for ten minutes or more, because by then you'll have established good blood flow to your brain. At that point, you'll find it relatively easy to figure out how to solve whatever problems you're facing.

Combining exercise and mindful awareness

Use the time you spend exercising as an opportunity to practise mindfulness. When you focus fully and completely on what you're doing as you move, you'll find that you'll move more adaptively and gracefully.

The dancer Akram Khan spoke of good movement most eloquently when he described Kathak, a type of Indian dancing. He said that the word 'katha' means 'story' in Sanskrit, and that he who tells a story is a 'katthaka'. He added that when he was learning to dance, his teachers told him to 'think of the space that you enter and work in as a temple.'

('Desert Island Discs', Radio 4, 22 July 2012)

In summary, when you move, try always to move thoughtfully. Find every opportunity you can to enhance your strength, endurance, flexibility and clarity of mind. Keep yourself well through movement and communicate a sense of calm and purpose when you move, as often as possible.

How to Move For Health

1. Use every opportunity to build movement into your life. When you're more active, you'll be healthier and you'll feel more able to solve the problems life throws at you.

2. Find an opportunity at least once every day to move steadily for 15 to 30 minutes. This will release endorphins and help you feel more calm and optimistic. There's no need to 'go for the burn': the key is steady, rather than quick, movement. Any aerobic activity will do – walking, jogging, dancing, cycling, swimming, gardening, doing housework or using any cardio machine.

3. Choose to move in ways that develop the four key aspects of good health: strength, endurance, flexibility, and clarity of mind.

REST

Adequate rest is essential for your wellbeing. When you rest, you give your body time to recover and, if necessary, to heal. Adequate rest also means that it will be easier for you to maintain a realistic perspective and solve the problems you'll inevitably encounter. That's because when you're rested, logic can prevail over emotional responses to frustration such as anger and impatience – the very feelings that may cause you to act unwisely.

Throughout this section I'll be talking about 'adequate rest', rather than 'adequate sleep'. This is deliberate. The most common cause of poor sleep is excessive worry, and an insomniac's most common worry is whether he'll sleep well on a given night! Anyone can decide to release some tension and become more relaxed – adequate rest is, therefore, an achievable goal. On the other hand, you can't 'make' yourself drift off to sleep. Therefore, the most realistic route to feeling calm – particularly if you have trouble sleeping well – is to reassure yourself that you'll allow ample opportunity for rest, and that will give you the strength to carry on. At the same time, trust your body's wisdom: when you really need sleep, your body will respond to that need.

Discovering how much rest is enough for you

At first glance, this appears to be a tricky question to answer because there's so much disagreement. If you ask a group of people how much sleep/rest they require to feel at their best, individuals will report anything between four to ten hours, with seven to eight hours being the most common response. To make matters more complicated, this figure varies for a given individual depending on their age, the time of year and their current activity level.

A much more accurate and helpful way to answer this question is to think in terms of sleep cycles. The notion of a sleep cycle developed out of the work of two American researchers, Dr Nathaniel Kleitman and Dr William C. Dement, in the mid-50s. They discovered that by measuring brainwaves, they could identify when an individual was dreaming. This became known as 'REM', or Rapid Eye Movement sleep. This led them to understand that sleep does not consist of a single state, but is instead made up of a series of sleep cycles. Each sleep cycle consists of three main states: light sleep, deep sleep and REM sleep. They found that before a REM episode begins, the individual will wake up briefly. However, unless you are anxious or uncomfortable, you're unlikely to remember that you woke at those times.

The length of an individual's sleep cycle is between about one and a half to two and a half hours, and that length remains consistent throughout your lifetime. What does change – depending on your age and circumstances – is the *number* of sleep cycles you'll need to feel rested. It's also the case that you'll feel more rested if you wake naturally – that is, just before a REM episode – than if you are awakened at other times. Therefore, if you know the length of your sleep cycle, you can arrange to go to bed and get up at times that will help you feel more rested.

The most accurate way to discover this is to spend the night in a sleep laboratory, so that researchers can measure your brainwaves. This is, obviously, not something most of us will want or have the opportunity to do! There is, however, another and much simpler way to determine the length of your own sleep cycle. You need to choose three nights when you don't have to get up at a particular time the next morning. These nights need not be consecutive, so for most of us that would mean choosing three or four weekend dates. Here's what to do:

Keeping a sleep cycle diary

Choose three nights within the next month when you need not get up at a particular time the next morning. Keep a pen and paper within reach when you're in bed and make sure there's a clock in your bedroom near your bed where it's easy for you to see it.

Whenever you wake during the night, jot down the time.

As soon as you wake the next morning, record the following:

1. *What time you got into bed*

2. *What time you last remember being awake (this needn't be exact)*

3. *Any times you woke in the night, together with why you woke up and the approximate time it took you to fall asleep again. (That is, the time you remember*

noticing before you fell asleep again. This is an exercise in approximation, and that's fine!)

4. *What time you woke up in the morning*

5. *How rested you felt when you get up, based on a 0 to 100 rating where 0 means you're not rested at all and 100 means you're totally rested*

Add up the total time you slept during that night.

Now take a look at the reasons you woke during the night, if there were any such times. Eliminate those occasions when you woke because something disturbed you, i.e. you were startled by a loud noise in the street or there was a sudden storm, for example. You'll want to consider only those occasions when you woke naturally, for example, because you had to go to the loo.

Take a look at each time you woke naturally. Subtract the time you woke up from the time you last fell asleep. So say you fell asleep about 12 and then woke at 3 a.m. to go to the loo. You then fell asleep again about 3.20 a.m. and woke up once again just before 8. You will, therefore, record two sleep periods, one three hours long and the other four and a half hours in length.

Most of you will record between two and five time intervals each night. Once you have the figures for three nights you'll be able to figure out the length of your sleep cycle as follows.

Compare the various 'sleep periods' to find a common divisor. You can do this either by taking an average of the figures (add them all together then divide by the number of intervals), or more simply by looking at them to see what number between 1.5 and 2.5 hours (the most common length for a sleep cycle) divides best into all of them.

Let's try another example. Say you went to bed at 10 p.m. and last remember noticing the time at 10.30 p.m. You then woke at just after 3 a.m. to go to the loo and fell asleep again at about 3.20 a.m. You woke again at 4.45 a.m., although you weren't sure why, and last remember that the time was 5.30 a.m. You then woke up, ready for the day ahead, at 8.30 a.m.

Your intervals are, therefore, 4 hours 30 minutes (10.30 p.m. to 3 a.m.), 1 hour 25 minutes (3.20 a.m. to 4.45 a.m.), and 3 hours (5.30 a.m. to 8.30 a.m.). Your sleep cycle is most likely to be 1.5 hours, because no other figure between 1.5 and 2.5 divides as neatly into all three of those intervals.

Once you know your sleep cycle length you'll be able to ensure that you're as rested as possible, no matter how late you stay up or how early you have to get up in the morning. In other words, if you sleep/rest for a period of time that adds up to a number of *complete* sleep cycles for you, you'll feel more awake and rested than you will if you're awakened in the middle of one of your sleep cycles – no matter how long you've been asleep.

Although the ideal number of sleep cycles for most adults is three or four, it's still more restful to wake at the end of any number of full sleep cycles than it is to stay in bed for longer. Here's an example to explain what I mean:

You know that your sleep cycle is two hours. On a particular night, you meet a friend for supper and you don't get back until just before midnight. You know from your sleep diary that you need about 30 minutes to get off to sleep. You also know that you have to get up at 7 a.m. the next morning to get ready for work. Therefore, if you go to bed straight away at midnight – thus resting/sleeping for 6.5 hours, from 12.30 a.m. to 7 a.m. – you'll be *more* tired than if you stay up for another half an hour. If you wait to go to bed at 12.30 a.m., you'll fall asleep around 1 a.m. and you'll therefore have had six hours of rest (three full sleep cycles) when your alarm goes off at 7 a.m.

At times, you may be tempted to try to 'make up' for lost sleep by lying in at the weekend. Sadly, unless you're a growing child or adolescent, this will only make you feel more tired rather than less. This is because humans are creatures of habit. If you go to bed at about the same time each night and wake at around the same time each morning, then you may feel temporarily disorientated if you change your schedule.

However, disorientation isn't necessarily a 'bad' feeling! The way you choose to interpret what's going on is far more important than when you get up, or what time you go to bed. Therefore, if you oversleep unintentionally – or for that matter, even if you get up late because you decided to have a lie-in – then if you decide to feel guilty about this you'll interpret any unusual feelings to be proof that you've done something wrong. If instead you either shrug your shoulders and decide you needed the sleep, or choose to enjoy a lazy day, any disorientation will soon disappear. It is definitely all in the mind!

That said, you will always feel less rested if you wake in the middle of a sleep cycle than if you wake at the end of a full cycle, whatever time you wake up.

Other factors that determine the need for rest

In addition to respecting the length of your sleep cycle, there are several other factors that will make a difference as well. It's a good idea to make allowances for these, particularly if you've already figured out your sleep cycle length and have made use of that knowledge but you still feel tired when you get up. The most important factors are these:

Time of year

Nowadays, we run our timetables without regard to season. However, this has not always been so. Archaeological evidence suggests that until relatively recently, before electricity was readily available to give us artificial heat and lighting, people stayed in bed far longer during the winter months than they did during the spring and summer. Some researchers estimate that people may have stayed in bed for as much as 18 of every 24 hours in winter! Like most mammals, humans have traditionally respected and worked with the seasons, being more active and mobile when it's light and warm and less so when it's dark and cold. Our brains are designed to respond favourably to light, allowing us to feel more inclined to be active during daylight hours.

Furthermore, although modern conveniences allow us to continue our normal activities even when it's cold and dark, we generally use more energy during the winter months. That's because whenever we go outside in the winter, we burn extra energy simply keeping warm.

Therefore, for reasons of both light and temperature, it's natural for us to need more rest during the winter months than we do during the summer.

Age

The second factor to consider when you determine how much rest you need is your age. Although the *length* of your sleep cycle doesn't change during your lifetime, the *number* of cycles you'll need to feel rested may do.

Infants, for example, need eight to ten cycles, or around 16 hours of sleep each day. The amount we need then diminishes with age until puberty, when it rises again before settling to between three and five cycles, or seven to nine hours each day during the first part of our adult lives. As we grow older our need for rest appears to decrease further, sometimes to as little as only one or two cycles each day. However, this apparent decrease may have more to do with your expectations and level of activity than it does about the physiology of ageing.

That's because in the past, older people were expected to do less and it may be their inactivity that created less need for rest, rather than their age. Therefore, in the future, because older people are remaining well and active for longer, we may not see a decrease in the amount of rest an individual needs as he or she ages.

There's a further complication in terms of age and rest needed. Children, adolescents and young adults seem able to compensate for a sleepless night by sleeping longer during the next few days. Sadly, however, this approach doesn't appear to benefit anyone beyond the age of about 30. That's why teenagers insist that they benefit from weekend 'lie-ins', whereas adults tend to feel even more tired if, after a hectic week, they stay in bed late at the weekend. For the latter, a short nap within 24 hours of a bad night is the best way to feel refreshed, rather than attempting to 'add hours' to the night's sleep several days later.

Individual diurnal variation

Another important factor when you're looking for ways to ensure that you're as rested as possible is to think about the times of day when you're most likely to be tired vs. when you most enjoy being active.

Some people are 'larks' – that is, they find it easy to get up early but difficult to stay awake at night. Others are 'owls' – they're wide awake at night, but seldom keen to get out of bed early in the morning. I refer to this as a 'natural' propensity, because it's not clear whether it's a genetic given or the result of long-established habits. Whichever it is, what is well known is that this tendency is almost impossible to change in adult life. Therefore, it's better to work with your natural inclination than it is to try to fight against it.

Level of activity

The more physically active you are, the more sleep and rest you'll need. However, there's a paradox here: the more physically active you are, the more likely you are to fall asleep quickly and to feel clear-headed and refreshed when you wake up. Therefore, if you take time regularly to exercise, although you'll then have less time to do other things, the time you will have will be of a higher 'quality' because you'll be able to focus and think more clearly.

Chronic stress levels

The more often you feel stressed, the more rest and sleep you'll need. However, there's a paradox under these circumstances as well, just as there is with regard to physical activity. Although you need more rest when you're under stress, you'll find it difficult to relax fully or to fall asleep quickly during stressful times. Moreover, because you rarely have the opportunity to feel calm and relaxed, you're unlikely ever to feel rested, no matter how many hours you spend in bed.

You can combat this feeling of constant weariness to some extent by taking 'power' naps (see page 90). However, in the longer term, the best way to deal with high levels of stress is to figure out ways to reduce or avoid them, even if that means you have to make some dramatic decisions about the way you live and work.

Tips to help the insomniac

Insomnia is a common and debilitating problem – in fact, GPs list it as one of the most common reasons patients make appointments to see them. If you're one of the many individuals who finds it difficult to relax and get off to sleep at night, don't despair! If you've already done all you can to decrease the stress levels you habitually face during the day and despite your efforts you're not sleeping well, there are still a number of things you can do to improve the quality of your sleep. Here are some suggestions:

1. *Bedtime routines*

   Take a careful look at your 'winding down' routine at night. It's important to establish a bedtime routine that's familiar, relaxing and comforting. You might, for example, take a warm bath or shower, lower the lights, fix yourself a cup of herbal tea or hot chocolate, and read something you enjoy. Then spend at least five minutes practising mindful breathing.

2. *Reduce distractions*

   Be sure to turn off all screens at least 30 minutes before you plan to go to bed. Screen-based activity will encourage you to feel distracted, and anything but calm. If you're easily awakened by light, consider putting some heavy curtains in your bedroom, those made from material that blocks out light. If noise is a problem, look into either using earplugs if you can tolerate them comfortably, or purchasing a white noise fan. This equipment is available in most pharmacies.

3. *Create a 'worry notebook'*

If you have a tendency to worry – especially at night – make yourself a 'worry notebook'. At least half an hour before you wish to get into bed, write down everything that's making you feel anxious. Make some notes as well about what you could do tomorrow to alleviate your worries. Be sure you do this somewhere outside the bedroom, so you don't associate your bedroom with worrying, and leave the worry book outside your bedroom when you've finished writing. If, once you've settled in bed, you think of other worries and you don't feel able to dismiss them, get up and record them – in your notebook and in the other room – and then go back to bed.

You'll find that after only a few nights, your worry list will begin to decrease. That's because worries, although they may seem numerous, tend to revolve around only a few particular themes. These are most often your health, your children, or your financial situation. Once you become aware of your particular worry theme or themes and you start to see that many of your 'different' worries are one and the same, problem solving will begin to feel simpler and you'll relax. That in turn will make it easier for you to generate realistic solutions.

4. *Use power naps*

There will be times when, despite all your good intentions, you'll get up knowing that you're not as rested as you'd like to be. On those days, a power nap is a wonderful way to restore your vitality. You need to find only ten minutes, but those ten minutes will be worth over an hour of sleep at night. Power naps can also help you 'in advance' – that is, when you're planning a night out and you know you won't have much time for bed rest that night.

- Here's what you do:
- Find a quiet place that's warm but not hot or stuffy and somewhere you're not likely to be interrupted. Turn off all communication devices.
- Lie down on the floor, your head resting on a book or a firm pillow, knees bent comfortably and a hip width apart, with arms 'flopped' at your sides. Alternatively, you can sit in a comfortable chair, with your arms in your lap or resting on the arms of the chair.
- Set an alarm, or ask someone to let you know when 10 minutes have elapsed.
- Now, simply close your eyes and breathe evenly and slowly, in through your nose and out through your mouth. As thoughts arise, observe them but don't judge them or attempt to make any decisions. Simply allow your thoughts to drift in and out of awareness.
- You needn't fall asleep. Simply let go and relax. When the 10 minutes are up, roll onto your side and sit up slowly. You're then free to continue your normal activities.

- You can take up to two power naps each day and still gain the maximum benefit. In this way, each power nap is the equivalent to one full cycle of sleep at night.

5. *Use a light alarm or a light box*

   There are a significant number of individuals who find it difficult to get out of bed during the winter months, even when they allow themselves extra sleep. They're also more likely to feel depressed at that time of year. These individuals are particularly responsive to light and the condition they suffer from is known as Seasonal Affective Disorder, or SAD. It seems that this problem is part of an individual's biological makeup so, if you suffer from SAD, you'll probably need to accept your sensitivity and learn to work with it, rather than to deny it. There are several things you can do to lift your mood and raise your energy levels during the winter. Here are some suggestions:

   - Make sure you get outside in natural light for at least 20 minutes every day. You'll find that this will lift your mood even on cloudy days. Talk to your doctor about the level of sunscreen you may need to use.

   - Buy a light alarm or a light box. These can be obtained by post or by searching on the internet. A light box is a device that you sit in front of for 20 to 30 minutes a day; the light alarm gives off increasing light during the half hour before you wake up. Either will give you the equivalent of a 'dose' of sunlight and users generally feel more alert, and also more optimistic and cheerful after exposure.

- Organise your holidays so that you take your main holiday during the winter months. Spend the time somewhere that has more daylight hours than where you're living. This can boost your spirits and outlook, to help you get through the short winter days.

6. *Learn not to fight sleepless nights*
   There may be some nights when, whatever you do, you'll find that you're unable to sleep. You may be under extreme pressure, or worried about a loved one – or sometimes, there will be no apparent reason for your wakefulness.

   Rather than staying in bed, 'trying' to fall asleep, it's better on those occasions simply to get up and leave the bedroom. This avoids setting up an association between wakefulness and your bed. Here are some ways you can use that time to restore a sense of calm:

   - Try sitting down in another room and writing out the thoughts that are keeping you awake. Once you feel you've 'emptied your mind', go back to bed and try breathing slowly and evenly, in through your nose and out through your mouth.
   - If, however, over half an hour elapses and you're still wide awake, it's best to get up and leave the bedroom again. Go somewhere you associate with comfort and good feelings – the kitchen, perhaps, or your sitting room. Fix a cup of sweet herbal tea if that appeals. If you're hungry, fix yourself a light snack, selecting foods that will help you relax such as a banana or a milky drink.

- Now choose a relaxing activity, something you enjoy but also something that's not particularly challenging. You might, for example, read an entertaining novel or listen to the radio or your favourite CD. Avoid turning on the TV or your computer, because screen work will make you feel more awake and distracted. Make sure you're warm and comfortable.

- Many of my clients who suffer from insomnia establish a 'sanctuary', a particular place in the house that they love, where tea-making equipment, a comfortable chair, reading material and a radio – but *not* a TV! – are already right there. Such a place will feel instantly cosy and comfortable, and help you relax more quickly.

- Stay up until you feel sleepy and only then go back to bed. Once you're back in bed, breathe in slowly and evenly. If by any chance you don't drift off, or at least feel truly relaxed and comfortable after about half an hour, get up and return to your special place until you feel ready to return to bed again.

You may worry that, if you get out of bed when you can't sleep, you'll lose even more sleep. In the short term, that's probably right. However, within a few weeks you'll begin to sleep more soundly and restfully in your bed, because you'll have broken the association between your bed and a time to lie awake worrying. You will have created a new association between being in bed and feeling relaxed and sleepy.

How to Benefit Most When You Rest

1. Discover the length of your sleep cycle and estimate how long it generally takes you to fall asleep at night, so you can get the most out of your sleeping time. The average adult needs three or four sleep cycles of rest to feel best, although that depends on certain factors such as the individual's age, diurnal variation, stress and activity levels, and the time of year.

2. Establish a comforting and pleasant bedtime routine and stick to it as often as possible. In particular, be sure to stop all screen-based activity within 30 minutes of getting into bed.

3. To ensure serenity and clarity of mind even during periods when you know it will be difficult to sleep adequately, take up to two power naps each day.

4. If you suffer from SAD, use a light box or light alarm to lift your spirits and help you feel more alert. If possible, spend some time away during the winter somewhere where there are more daylight hours.

5. If you lie awake for more than half an hour, get up and comfort yourself with a light snack and/or a non-caffeinated drink. Read something soothing or listen to the radio until you feel tired, then return to your bed.

NUTRITION

If you start looking for advice to help you decide what diet is best for you, no doubt you'll feel instantly overwhelmed. There are literally thousands of books to choose from. To make your decision even more difficult, you'll soon discover that much of the advice that's offered is contradictory and, even worse, that it is constantly changing.

The overall effect, in my opinion, is quite damaging. What this avalanche of information suggests is that there's no 'gold standard' when it comes to defining good nutrition. There's a second, extremely demeaning implication as well and that is that no one but the professionals are capable of figuring out which diet is best for you.

I couldn't disagree more strongly with the latter implication. Although you may know less about food science than most nutritionists and diet doctors, none of them know as much about your particular body as you do. Therefore, it's important always to consider your own reactions to the foods or diets you're encouraged to try and to value your reaction every bit as highly as you do the suggestions from professionals.

The difficulty, however, is that most of the time you probably don't stop to think about how particular foods taste, how they make you feel, or what effect they have on your clarity of mind.

When you become mindful, however, that will change. Mindful awareness allows you to get in touch with your own good sense and to become aware of the effect that different foods have on you. Therefore, what you've learned in Step One will help you determine which foods make you feel anxious, distractable or guilty, and which help you to feel calm and relaxed.

The truth is, each of us is unique, so there's no one special diet that will suit everyone. Therefore, I invite you to create your own. To help you, I'll share what's known about the relationship between diet and human stress levels.

Let's start with the golden rule when it comes to selecting healthy foods:

The closer a food is to its natural state, the more confident you can feel that it's worth incorporating into your diet. On the other hand, the more it's been altered – that is, refined, processed, or 'enhanced' with chemicals – the more cautious you should be about eating a great deal of it.

Now let's turn to the specific issues that will help you use what you eat to ensure that you're as healthy and calm as possible, both in body and in mind.

Negotiating the minefield of information

There's so much written about diet and nutrition yet, despite the volume of literature, there's little agreement among the experts. This lack of unity could make you feel lost and uncertain and stressed, it's true. However, another way of looking at this state of affairs is that it's very freeing for you. To create your optimal diet you need do only two things.

First, acquaint yourself with what's reasonably well established in the field of nutrition. In this section, I've attempted to assist you with this by offering suggestions that are backed up by solid research and that have stood the test of time.[1]

Once you've read through this section it's time for the second step: creating your own optimal diet. Choose the foods that appeal to you based on what you've learned, and then try them out using mindful awareness to decide which work best for you.

One of the most freeing aspects of this new attitude to diet is that you can forget all about measuring, weighing, and trying to determine a 'healthy' portion size. Instead, if you'll take time to notice what you're eating, and how it makes you feel (rather than eating while doing any number of other things, as most of us do), you'll start to discover for yourself what foods are best for you.

Making informed choices

The best way to choose a healthy diet for you is to start by familiarising yourself with the way nutritionists

---

1 It is important to note that this section gives you a succinct overview of dietary recommendations but I don't go into great detail in the text about the composition of each food or the specific studies on which I'm basing my suggestions. If you wish to find out more, you can find that information by accessing the sources listed in the index.

categorise different foods. You can then decide which categories, and which foods within those categories, are most likely to help you feel healthy, alert and calm, and which are more likely to leave you feeling irritable, tense and distracted.

The foods we eat, as you probably know already, are grouped into three main categories – proteins, carbohydrates and fats. You need foods from all three of these categories to maintain good health, although there is disagreement among nutritionists and diet doctors about how much of each food group is best.

Proteins are primarily used by the body for maintenance, for keeping your muscles and organs in good repair, and throughout childhood and adolescence for promoting growth. Proteins also contain minerals and other trace elements that are vital for both mental and physical health and help to stabilise blood glucose levels. This is important for keeping your energy levels on an even keel. Proteins are abundant in meat, fish, eggs and dairy products. Nuts, unrefined carbohydrates and pulses also contain some protein.

The second category is fats. You eat fats primarily to supply energy although they also contain micronutrients, particularly in fatty acids, that are necessary for good brain functioning. Fats are, however, an extremely concentrated source of calories, so it's best to eat them in smaller quantities than you do proteins or carbohydrates. Fats generally accompany proteins and carbohydrates; they're rarely eaten on their own.

Carbohydrates make up the third category. Grains, cereals, pulses, vegetables, fruits and sugars – both refined and unrefined – all fall into this group. Carbohydrates are our main source of energy, the provider of fuel for your brain as well as your muscles. Carbohydrates are generally digested more quickly than fats or proteins, although there's huge variation among foods in this group. The speed at which a carbohydrate breaks down to become energy for your body depends on the type of sugar it contains and to what degree it's been refined.

Unless you have a specific food intolerance or allergy, the best guide to healthy eating is to make sure you include as wide a variety of wholesome foods in your diet as possible. That way, you're most likely to get all the nutrients, vitamins and minerals that your body needs.

Eating to beat stress

To help you create and maintain a sense of calm and stabilise your mood, the key is always to include some complex carbohydrates when you eat. They'll be better absorbed if you eat them with a small amount of protein – so for example, an excellent calming snack would be a slice of bread with some nut butter, a bowl of pasta with a sprinkling of cheese, or an apple or banana together with a handful of almonds.

You can be even more certain that you're choosing calming foods if you look for carbohydrates that are particularly rich in B vitamins. The B vitamins are often referred to as 'nature's tranquillisers'. They're abundant in whole grains, wheatgerm, nuts, eggs and dairy products. Live yogurt is particularly helpful. So for example, an excellent way to start your day with a calm and focused state of mind would be to enjoy a bowl of muesli with nuts and live yogurt.

Iron and magnesium are also important for stabilising your mood. The richest sources of magnesium are nuts. Peanut butter on a slice of wholemeal bread makes an excellent calming snack. Iron can be obtained by eating meat, eggs, dark green leafy vegetables, apricots and whole grains. Therefore, another way to start your day calmly would be to eat scrambled eggs and a slice of wholegrain toast for breakfast.

Foods that contain serotonin also encourage a sense of calm and contentment. Examples of serotonin-rich foods are bananas, figs, dates, pineapples, walnuts and avocados. These choices make particularly good snacks.

Finally, don't forget to include some calming, mood-enhancing herbs when you're preparing meals. These include rosemary, basil, thyme and nutmeg.

Foods to avoid or to treat with care

The number one enemy of calm is any refined carbohydrate. Sucrose or table sugar, or any foods that contain them such as cakes and sweets, will deliver an enormous 'hit' of energy but then leave you feeling depleted. This in turn will cause you to feel agitated and you'll find it difficult to concentrate. Refined carbohydrates are also problematic because they create cravings. Instead of feeling calm and able to get on with your day, these foods will leave you feeling dissatisfied, distracted and probably thinking you're hungrier than you were before you ate them. Therefore, it's best to avoid sugar and sugar-based foods whenever you can.

Avoid drinking copious amounts of tea and coffee, as well as soft drinks that contain caffeine. Taken in excess, the caffeine in them can make you feel anxious and twitchy and may interfere with your ability to sleep as well. If you enjoy hot drinks, you could try herbal tea instead. Fennel and peppermint, taken together, makes a particularly soothing drink and can also aid digestion.

Finally, go easy on alcohol. You may think of alcohol as a relaxant but in fact it's a depressant. It's also dehydrating and this can cause cloudy thinking and create a sense of confusion. Alcohol also breaks down B vitamins and magnesium, the very substances that help you most when you wish to feel calm.

Eating for energy and endurance

Energy levels are intimately connected to one's sense of wellbeing. When you know you have the energy to do the things you want and need to do, it's easy to feel calm and confident. When, however, your energy levels are either consistently low or unpredictably up and down, you'll feel stressed and out of control. Therefore, it's extremely important to eat in ways that deliver consistent, steady energy. Here's how:

- Eat something at frequent and regular intervals. Your blood glucose levels will start to drop between three and four hours after you eat. You can avoid energy dips, therefore, if you have a healthy meal or snack every three to four hours throughout the day.

- Eat your first meal as soon after waking as you can manage comfortably. Some of us can eat straight away on rising; others may need an hour or even two before feeling hungry. Remember that, to a large extent, when you first feel hungry is a product of habit. Therefore, if you've never eaten breakfast, you can change your ways and cultivate a healthier habit. You could try drinking something nourishing, perhaps a fruit and yogurt smoothie in the morning, rather than trying to eat something straight away. Or you could start small, perhaps eat just a banana and then gradually add some yogurt or cereal to your breakfast. Eating early in the day has been shown to be important if you want to keep your energy levels steady throughout your waking hours.

- Make sure you drink enough water. One of the first signs of dehydration is feeling tired, and many people mistakenly believe they lack sleep when in fact they just need a glass of water! It's particularly important to drink a glass or two on rising because you lose a great deal of water throughout the night, particularly if you sleep in a warm room. If you have children, make sure they start the day with some water too. A recent survey suggested that over half of all schoolchildren in England go to school mildly dehydrated, and that may impair their ability to pay attention and learn. The amount of water you need each day varies of course depending on how active you are, the air temperature, and your weight. However, a good rough guide is to make sure you drink about six glasses of water in any 24 hour period. Other drinks are great if you like them, but they should be considered an addition to the water you drink if you want to avoid feeling tired.

- Just as you would to ensure a sense of calm, make sure that each meal or snack you have is balanced, so it contains some complex carbohydrates plus a bit of protein and fat. When energy levels are your main concern, however, choose your fats and your carbohydrates carefully. The best fats are unsaturated because they're easier to digest. The best carbohydrates are those that have a medium or medium to low glycaemic index, or GI rating. Make sure you eat plenty of foods that contain Omega 3 fatty acids. These fatty acids boost blood flow, and that in turn helps you think more clearly. Omega 3 fatty acids are found most abundantly in fish and shellfish, tofu, avocados, walnuts and green leafy vegetables.

The GI index measures carbohydrates according to their effect on your blood sugar levels. Those foods with lower ratings – for our purposes, under about 60 – will break down more steadily in your body. These foods are, therefore, unlikely to spike your energy levels and cause you to endure alternating peaks and dips of energy.

The GI index is therefore a useful way to categorise food if your energy levels are a concern. It's easy to get hold of a GI guide. Do, however, take care not to let such ratings start to become yet another source of stress! It's easy to become overly concerned with this index. The wisest approach is to make a list of those foods – in particular, the complex carbohydrates – that you love and that you know are good for you, and acquaint yourself with their relative GI ratings. Then, if you notice that you've been feeling lethargic, make sure you choose to eat more of your low GI favourites as opposed to any others. So, for example, an apple or pear together with some walnuts or a carton of plain yogurt would make a better pick-me-up than would a slice of fruit cake or even most 'health bars'. The latter almost always contain lots of sugar.

You can learn more about the GI Index at www.weightlossresources.co.uk/diet/gi. Another useful resource is *GI: How to Succeed Using a Glycaemic Index Diet*, published by HarperCollins.

When your 'hunger' isn't physical

There will be times when, no matter what you eat or how much of it you eat, you'll still feel empty and unsettled. At those times, you're probably not physically hungry. Once you've provided your body with adequate nutrition – provided of course that you didn't fill up on sugary foods, which would induce cravings rather than satisfy hunger – you should feel comfortable and content.

To test whether your hunger is physical, stop eating and go somewhere that doesn't remind you of food or food preparation. Choose an activity you enjoy and preferably one that's also moderately challenging. For example, you might do some gardening. If you play a musical instrument, learn a new piece. Telephone a friend you've not spoken to in a long time, ask them what they've been doing, and listen – really listen and pay full attention. Continue with this pursuit for 20 minutes or more. Then if you still feel hungry, you probably really are physically hungry. Feel free to fix yourself a healthy snack consisting mainly of low GI carbohydrate food and eat it mindfully.

Chances are, however, you'll no longer feel hungry after 'feeding' your mind.

It's easy to mistake feeling bored or lonely or under-challenged with feeling physically hungry because, for most of us, this was the first habit we developed. As a baby, when you cried, what do you suppose was your parent's first reaction? Generally, when a baby cries, a carer will try feeding it first before even considering any other possible reason.

Therefore, whenever you feel unaccountably 'hungry', take a moment and allow yourself to become mindfully aware. Is the feeling entirely a physical sensation or are you 'hungry' for something other than food – company or perhaps a new challenge? Step Three will help you get to know yourself better so next time you feel that sort of hunger, you'll be able to choose from one of many more creative and fulfilling ways to satisfy yourself.

How to Eat For Best Health

1. Dietary advice is constantly changing and often contradicting itself. Instead of following the latest fad or diet, learn to trust your own sense of what's best for you. You can do this most effectively by learning to eat mindfully – that is, to focus fully on what you're eating and not to do other things at the same time.

2. Eat a wide variety of wholesome foods to maximise the chance that you'll obtain all the nutrients, vitamins and minerals that your body needs.

3. As often as possible, choose foods that are in their natural state, as opposed to those that have been refined, processed or 'enhanced' with artificial ingredients.

4. Try to eat at regular intervals to keep your energy levels steady – every three to four hours during the day.

5. To help stabilise mood and energy levels, keep sucrose (refined sugar) to a minimum and avoid excessive amounts of alcohol and caffeine.

6. Avoid becoming dehydrated. Drinking water will help keep your mind clear.

7. Use mindful awareness to distinguish between physical and psychological hunger, and discover the healthiest ways to satisfy each.

Step Three:
Know Yourself

'Knowing yourself is the beginning of all wisdom'
Aristotle

Like a snowflake, each of us is unique. We are also incredibly complex and we become increasingly more so as we grow older.

Yet how often do you stop to think about the many sides of your character, the many different roles you play each day and the differing talents and skills you have at your disposal? You probably think of yourself as behaving consistently, when in fact you fulfil a number of different roles in different situations, and you're many different things to different people.

One of the most serious problems today is how prone we are to undervaluing ourselves and to underestimating our possibilities. As you steam through your busy day, I suspect that you rarely stop to think whether you really need to do everything you feel you should do, or whether what you're doing is making the best use of your skills and talents. Therefore, you need to gain a clear idea of just who you really are, so you'll know where your talents lie and how and where you can use your abilities most effectively. That's what you'll discover in this step.

We'll begin with your personality. What are your strongest characteristics? What are your vulnerabilities? For example, are you an extrovert or an introvert? Are you conscientious or disorganised? Optimistic or pessimistic? I will explain which of these characteristics you were born with – they're the ones you'll want to respect and work with, rather than try to fight against. Other characteristics may have a genetic component, but your experiences will also have played a part – what you learned from your parents, how your birth order position influenced what happened to you, and the effects of various early experiences. As a result of those experiences you developed habits, and if you wish to do so you can always change your habits, no matter how deeply ingrained you believe them to be.

Just as you learned in Step One to override the habit of rushing mindlessly through your day, so you can also change other unwanted habits. Start by looking for the circumstances that trigger the behaviour or attitude you wish to change. Next, decide in clear and concrete terms how you would prefer to react. Work towards your new way of being in small steps, practising each step often, until it feels comfortable to react in the new way. Then move on to the next step. Continue until your behaviour matches your ideal.

We'll turn to intelligence next. What are your strongest

abilities, and which subjects and skills do you find easiest to learn? Which ones feel like a constant struggle? Contrary to general belief, intelligence is not a unitary quality. Each of us is 'smart' in a number of different ways. I'll describe the six main types of intelligence and show you how to create your own 'smart profile'.

Finally, you'll reflect on your passions. What interests or pursuits have you always loved, even as a child? Which, when you begin them, allow you to become fully absorbed almost immediately, to forget where you are or how much time has passed? How could you integrate these passions more comprehensively into your life? This is not an indulgence – the things you love to do are the ones you'll do best, and the ones you'll continue to work at and to complete even in the face of obstacles and severe difficulties.

YOUR PERSONALITY

Your personality consists of those qualities that define the ways you think and behave, over time and in most situations. Of course, you'll show some qualities more freely in some circumstances than you will in others. For example, you might behave more assertively when you're with your brothers and sisters than when you're with your work colleagues. However, if a number of people who know you were asked whether, on balance, you're an assertive or a reserved individual, you'd no doubt find a fair amount of agreement among them.

Personality is made up of a number of dimensions – in fact, an unabridged English dictionary will contain almost 18,000 personality-relevant terms! These include descriptors such as rigidity, generosity, ambitiousness, honesty and so on. To some extent, the dimensions that you consider to be important will depend on the culture in which you grow up. So for example, Americans are likely to consider assertiveness to be more important than the British do.

A number of researchers, chief among them the British psychologist Raymond Cattell and the German psychologist Hans Eysenck, have attempted to simplify this enormous list, and over time some general agreement has emerged. Most psychologists now accept five main dimensions as the basis for describing all personalities.

The Big Five Personality Dimensions

- Extroversion-Introversion
- Neuroticism (or emotional stability/instability)
- Agreeableness
- Conscientiousness
- Openness to experience

Trying to visualise your personality is a bit like looking through that kaleidoscope once again, and at times it might seem like quite a challenge. You can get a feeling about the whole pattern straight away, whether it feels balanced or lop-sided, whether the various colours are powerful or whether they present an overall 'wash', whether the pattern feels complete or that somehow, there's something missing. You can turn the kaleidoscope – in terms of our analogy, you can imagine yourself in a different situation, with different people and a different set of responsibilities – and perhaps you will seem a different person. In fact, you're still the same person, but now different aspects of you are emphasised because the circumstances have changed, so in a way you seem different.

The qualities that make up your personality have come about as the result of nature – your own unique genetic makeup – and nurture – your experience. Although all characteristics owe their existence to both nature and nurture, some have been more highly influenced by one rather than the other. In particular, the two dimensions of introversion/extroversion and impulsive/reflective appear to be so heavily innate that it's better simply to accept them and use them to your best advantage, rather than to fight against them or try to change them. Later, I'll define these two dimensions and explain how you can use each to enhance the quality of your life.

All other aspects of your personality are more sensitive to environmental influence. They've come about as a result of experience generally, but particularly as a result of your childhood experiences – for example, how your parents raised you, whether you were a first, a middle, a last-born or an only child, your experiences at school, and when and how often you moved house.

Once you understand more clearly why you've come to be as you are, you have an exciting opportunity. You can now change the ways you behave whenever you choose to do so, because you know that much of your character has been learned. That's because anything that has been learned can be relearned more adaptively. All it takes is a willingness to be mindful of your own behaviour and then to choose to act in new ways.

What you will learn in this section will help you understand yourself better, and therefore to make wiser decisions in all sorts of areas of your life – in your career, in your choice of friends, and even when you choose a partner. With such knowledge you'll feel calmer, more self-confident and more certain that the choices you make will be the best ones for you.

THE TWO CHARACTERISTICS THAT ARE DIFFICULT TO CHANGE

You're no doubt familiar with these terms. Extroverts are the people who crave excitement. They often take chances and are prone to acting on the spur of the moment. They find it hard to motivate themselves to finish things and they tend to need deadlines to goad them into action. Extroverts work well in open plan offices and they enjoy working with other people. They generally have lots of friends and they love to party and to socialise generally.

Introverts, on the other hand, prefer to avoid excitement and pressure from outside. They tend to be reserved and thoughtful and are unwilling to make quick decisions. They work best in a quiet environment. Introverts are most comfortable with a few close friends rather than being part of a group. Some introverts actually dread crowds and will avoid big social gatherings at all costs.

Whether you're an extrovert or an introvert is evident from a very early age. Most psychologists agree that it has a genetic basis, and recently research has begun to decipher the neurochemical differences between introverts and extroverts. The psychoanalyst Carl Jung, a contemporary of Freud, was one of the first in his field to write about the introvert–extrovert dimension. He spoke of this dimension as being two parts of a whole. Jung believed that introverts and extroverts are attracted to one another because, he claimed, the presence of the opposite helps an individual feel stronger and more complete.

In the mid-1900s the psychologist Hans Eysenck became fascinated by the difference between introverts and extroverts. So pervasive was this aspect of human character that Eysenck believed it to be the most important dimension of personality. He also hypothesised that the difference between the two has a neurological basis. According to Eysenck, the reticular activating system, or RAS, is the part of the brain that determines the difference between extroverts and introverts. The RAS is the area that controls our arousal level – that is, our readiness to take action.

Eysenck claimed that introverts have a more active RAS, so they're by nature already highly stimulated and poised to act. The introvert doesn't, therefore, seek further encouragement to feel aroused. In fact, demands to meet deadlines as well as encouragement from others to socialise can easily feel overwhelming to the introvert, and they're likely to make him or her feel anxious.

On the other hand, Eysenck believed that extroverts are constitutionally understimulated. In other words, they have a relatively inactive RAS, so they need to obtain arousal from outside themselves. Extroverts therefore seek the very crowds and social gatherings that introverts try so hard to avoid.

In Western society today, extroverts are estimated to outnumber introverts at a ratio of about three to one. Furthermore, some psychologists have argued that the qualities possessed by extroverts are valued more highly than those of introverts. Those who defend introverts claim that we live in an 'extrovert world' and, as such, we only really value those who work well under pressure and who continually seek ever more demanding challenges.

My own experience suggests that extroverts probably do outnumber introverts in today's world. However, the idea that it's better to be an extrovert than an introvert is a more commonly held belief in America than it is in Europe.

If you want to know precisely how introverted or extroverted you are, you can do so by taking any one of a number of personality inventories. The one that's probably best known, if somewhat dated now, is Eysenck's original test, the Eysenck Personality Inventory, or EPI. It's made up of 57 short 'yes' or 'no' questions, and your eventual 'I-E score' indicates how strongly extroverted or introverted you are. If you wish to obtain a more precise indication of how introverted or extroverted you are, but at the same time you don't wish to go to the time and expense of taking a full personality inventory, there are a number of introversion/extroversion questionnaires you can find on the internet that will give you a numerical score. Two questionnaires you might like to try are:

www.thepowerofintroverts.com/quiet-quiz-are-you-an-introvert

www.funtestiq.com/personality/personalitytest39.shtml

However, you don't need to take a formal test to determine whether, as a general rule, you're more of an extrovert or more of an introvert. The descriptions given above are enough to allow you to decide.

Once you've made your decision, here's how you can use it to help you live a calmer and more fulfilling life.

If you're more extroverted than introverted

Friendships

You're at your best when you're with other people, so make sure there are plenty of opportunities for you to socialise. Because we tend to choose friends who share our interests, most of your friends will probably be extroverts as well and that means there's a danger that you could lose the necessary balance between energy expenditure and rest that all of us must have.

You'll need, therefore, to make sure you allow yourself opportunities to relax as well as to extend yourself. Your two daily mindful sessions will be invaluable in this respect. Not only will the five-minute periods be restorative in themselves, but each time you stop and ground yourself you'll also become aware of how you're feeling. If you notice that you're more tired than you want to be, take things at a slower pace for a while. In Step Four I'll give you advice on effectively saying 'no' to unnecessary, draining demands.

Although you'll naturally incline towards other extroverts, make sure that at least one good friend, or better yet your partner, is more introverted than you are. It will be easier that way to maintain balance in your life. Your partner will remind you of the need for quiet reflection, and you in turn will encourage them to reach out.

Work

You'll be happiest if you choose a job that involves lots of teamwork and plenty of social contact. Ask well in advance for timetables when what you're doing involves deadlines, and use Step Four to help you plan your work timetable effectively. That way, deadlines will serve as useful motivators for you rather than threats that make you feel overly stressed.

Taking care of yourself

Because extroverts love to act on the spur of the moment and take on opportunities the minute they arise, you may not know you're overdoing it until you're totally exhausted. Therefore, to make it less likely that you'll end up running on 'empty', it's very important to be strict with yourself about going to bed and getting up at a regular time.

Regular mealtimes are also important for the same reason. Avoid sweet drinks, sugary foods and excess caffeine. You don't need further encouragement to rush about! The advice in Step Two is thus even more important to remember.

Finally, taking regular exercise is unlikely to be a problem for you because extroverts enjoy action. However, be careful not to push yourself unnecessarily. For you, steady movement on a regular basis is more beneficial than bursts of intense exertion.

If you're more introverted than extroverted

Friendships

Introverts value their friendships just as much as do extroverts, but they're more particular about whom they choose as their friends. It's likely that you'll consider only a few people to be your real friends. This is lovely in one way, because you'll be able to find time to stay in touch with all of them. On the other hand, because there are so few, you may worry that you'll ask too much of any one of them.

Therefore, it's a good idea to consider 'levels' of friendship. It's fine to have only a very few close friends, but take time to stay in touch with those individuals you like, but whom you might not regard as 'close' friends as well.

Face-to-face contact will be more tiring for you than for an extrovert, but it's still just as important. That's because regular real human contact is vital for all of us. Therefore, make sure you meet up with a friend or acquaintance at least once every two weeks. In the meantime, emails and phone calls are less intense, so use these methods of staying in touch. Texting may be useful, but it won't help you feel as well connected.

Finally, as with extroverts, make sure one friend or your partner is quite unlike you with regard to this dimension. That way, you'll achieve the best balance in both your lives between expending and replenishing your energy.

Work

Whatever else you do, make sure there's a place at work

where you can retreat and have a bit of time on your own when you need to do so. You, unlike an extrovert, will need plenty of opportunities for 'down' time. Your retreat will have an added advantage because you'll have an ideal place to practise mindfulness.

Surprising though it may seem, it's better to work where there are others around you at least some of the time. Total isolation can cause you to lose perspective and ask too much of yourself, or to become 'stale' because there's no one else with whom you can share ideas.

Obviously, deadlines are unavoidable. Just like extroverts, you'll meet those deadlines with less stress if you know about them well in advance.

However, although you'll both benefit from advance notice, you'll do so in different ways. Whereas extroverts can use the imposed deadline as a basis to plan realistically, you'll be least stressed if you consider that deadline to be a 'fall-back'. Set your own deadline before the 'real' one and plan your schedule on that basis. This will allow you to feel more in control, and therefore less exposed to external stress.

Taking care of yourself

Most introverts are aware of their bodily state, so you'll probably know when you need to rest or to take a break from external stimulation. For you, power naps are a particularly powerful tool. Use Step Four to help you plan for regular 'time out' breaks. Regular bed times and waking times are helpful, particularly when those times respect the length of your sleep cycle. However, they won't help you as much as will short 'time out' breaks during the day.

You're also likely to be more aware than most of when you need to eat and drink. If you're going to be exposed to more environmental stress than usual, proteins will be particularly helpful because they break down more slowly in the body. When you need to concentrate for long periods, be sure to include plenty of complex carbohydrates.

Avoid overloading your system with large meals: eating often and moderately is best for you. Keep alcohol intake low, because you're likely to be very sensitive to its depressant effect.

Finally, you're less likely to feel like taking exercise than will an extrovert, because it can be perceived as stressful. However, it's important for you, because steady movement will help regulate your system and avoid unpleasant ups and downs. Think more about pacing than pushing – that is, go for steady, regular aerobic movement – and avoid over-taxing yourself.

Impulsive or reflective?

The other characteristic that appears to be highly consistent throughout our lives is how impulsive or reflective we are, both in our decisions and reactions as well as in our behaviour. As with introversion and extroversion, it's hard if not impossible to change your tendencies in this regard.

The Harvard psychologist Jerome Kagan has devoted much of his career to studying this aspect of human personality. He's discovered that even very young babies show impulsive or reflective behaviour reliably, lending weight to the probability that this is an inherited characteristic.

This dimension has a number of features in common with the introversion/extroversion dimension, and perhaps one day we'll find that they're closely linked neurologically. Eysenck was aware of the similarity – he described extroverts as 'impulsive' and introverts as those who 'look before they leap' – who are, in other words, reflective.

This dimension of personality contains vast variation in behaviour. There are those who are so highly impulsive that they're continually restless. They'll pounce on any new idea and react almost immediately to any new suggestion, only to move on to the next suggestion before carrying out any sustained action. At the other extreme, there are those who appear to be so lost in thought, so unable to make a decision, that they miss almost every opportunity they're given.

Most of us are, of course, somewhere in between these two extremes. If, on balance, you're more impulsive than you are reflective, you'll have a tendency to rush into action without stopping to think about the possible consequences. You'll rarely take time to consider all the disadvantages as well as the advantages of a particular decision before you act and, as a result, you're likely to make more mistakes than those who are more reflective. At the same time, however, because you're so quick off the mark, you manage to make use of more opportunities than those who insist on prior reflection. Finally, you may also find it difficult to concentrate because you have a tendency to jump from one idea to the next.

If on the other hand you're generally more reflective then, unlike your impulsive counterpart, you'll always try to think carefully before taking any action. You'll insist on considering all possibilities and evaluating their consequences before you make up your mind. You'll feel uncomfortable if you're hurried, and at times others may consider you to be slow or even stubborn. Although when you do make a decision you usually choose wisely, the cost of your deliberations is that you often miss out on opportunities because they've passed you by before you can make up your mind.

Once you've decided whether you're more impulsive or reflective, turn back to the guidelines given for introverted and extroverted personalities. If on balance you feel you're more reflective, follow the guidelines for the more introverted. If you feel that impulsive describes you more accurately, follow the suggestions for extroverted individuals.

Other dimensions of personality

The relative contributions of your genetics and your experience are more balanced across the remaining personality dimensions. So for example, how self-confident, ambitious, or cooperative you are owes at least as much to your past experience as to your genetic makeup. What that means is that, if you really want to change an attitude or a particular aspect of your behaviour, you can always do so. You simply need to identify clearly what you hope to change and make yourself aware of the circumstances that are most likely to trigger such behaviour. Next, describe to yourself – clearly and specifically – how you'd prefer to behave. From that time on, simply look out for your 'triggers' and remind yourself to think and act in the new ways. It won't be long before the new habit is well-established and takes precedence over older ways of behaving.

However, before you embark on any changes, think carefully *why* you wish to change. Is it because you hope to please someone who's important to you, or to make yourself appear more likeable and acceptable to others generally? If so, you'd be calmer and far happier in the long run if you stop trying to change in order to please other people and start accepting yourself as you are. Instead of endlessly criticising yourself and trying to act against your own tendencies in order to please everyone else, turn to Step Four and learn how to 'declutter psychologically'.

Environmental influences that help form character

You'll understand yourself better if you're aware of the major influences on character development. These are the factors that, when you were a child, caused you to think and behave as you do now. There are three of these factors.

- How you were parented,
- Your birth order position.
- Major events during childhood.

Let's look at each of these.

How you were parented

Human beings, more so than any other creature on earth, spend relatively more of their lives dependent on others of their own kind to care for them. In fact, until you were about five or six years old you depended completely on your carers to look after you. They were the most important people in your world, and your main aim was to please them so they'd continue to love you and to look after you. You were acutely aware of what pleased them and what didn't, and you reacted accordingly.

Furthermore, between the ages of about three and six, the period when we lay down the foundations of our identity, you copied almost everything they did or said. Your concept of what it means to be a male or a female, as well as how to be a mother or a father, was created during this time. Your sense of what's right and wrong, whether you're ambitious or cooperative, how generous you tend to be – all these characteristics and many more are based on the way your parents behaved around you when you were growing up.

In particular, there are three ways that your parents' attitudes and behaviour will have had a deep and profound effect on you. These are: how easy you find it to like and accept yourself as you are; how readily you can trust and like other people; and how easy it is for you to make adjustments when change is called for.

If your parents complimented you honestly, and if they praised you more often for showing effort and enthusiasm than for any prizes or accomplishments you may have achieved, then you'll find it easy as an adult to accept and like yourself. If on the other hand, they reserved their praise only for those occasions when you came top in the class or in some other way 'won' in comparison to others, then you'll have a tendency to push yourself extremely hard and you'll rarely feel satisfied with yourself.

If your parents, while maintaining a realistic view of the world and of the people around you, held an optimistic view on life generally, and if they tended to focus on the good in others rather than their faults, then you'll find it easy to feel relaxed and comfortable in most situations. If, instead, they complained often and frequently felt threatened or let down by others – and in particular if they had a tendency to find faults in others – then you'll feel less relaxed when meeting new people or entering new situations. Sadly, if they were overly trusting and were therefore taken advantage of by others, then you, too, may be overly gullible.

Finally, if your parents enjoyed new ventures and showed an open curiosity about whatever was going on in the world, then you'll find it relatively easy to welcome change in your life. If, however, they adhered rigidly to their routines, and if they reacted to change and new developments as if they were threatening, then you're likely to find it difficult to make changes yourself, and to adjust to new circumstances.

The problem with these fundamental attitudes is that they were largely formed before you were able to lay them down in words. They are, therefore, lodged deep within you, so it can feel like they're an innate part of you. They're not. They're learned behaviours that have become deeply ingrained habits, and therefore you can change them if you really wish to do so.

However, changing attitudes that are so very fundamental and deep-rooted is likely to require some very hard and sustained effort on your part. Therefore, you need to think carefully about whether such an undertaking would be worthwhile. Remember, if you wish to maintain a sense of inner peace and calm in your life, then any changes you choose to make *must* be based on your own concept of how *you* wish to live. If you wish to change only so that other people will approve of you or will like you better, then you'll continue to feel anxious and stressed – no matter how much you change.

Your birth order position

Your parents will have been enormously influential in your development because of their importance to your survival and comfort in early life. However, no influence on your development will be as long-lasting as your relationship with your siblings and your position relative to them in your family.

It's helpful to be aware of the factors that have shaped your character, because when you're able to understand more clearly why you've come to behave and think as you do, it will feel easier to accept yourself. There are, after all, good reasons why you think and act as you do!

Whether you were a first-born, a middle-born, a last-born or a single child will have an enormous impact on your character. Let's examine how, starting with first-borns.

First-borns

If you're a first-born, you're the only child in a family who enjoyed the undivided attention of your carers, only to lose it later to your new brother or sister. As a result, you are likely to grow up feeling incredibly determined to regain lost attention. You probably tried to please your parents by studying hard and doing well in school because this is often the first things parents will notice and praise in their children, and also by helping them manage their growing family. It's therefore no surprise that first-borns are most likely to occupy positions of authority and leadership – the positions that demand long study and unwavering determination to succeed – and to choose careers that involve nurturing – for example, to become teachers, doctors and nurses.

As the first-born, you will have had the benefit of being the sole object of your parents' care and attention for a time. That means you were held, attended to and talked to a great deal, almost certainly more than any of your younger siblings. You'll have had more opportunities to hear language and to observe adult, mature social interactions. What that means for you now is that you are probably well able to communicate clearly and relate skilfully to other people. You probably did fairly well in school, and of course this was no doubt rewarded by parental praise and approval.

At the same time, however, your parents were new at parenting and that's likely to mean that they were more nervous when they cared for you than they were, as subsequently more experienced parents, with your brothers and sisters. Because babies and children are acutely sensitive to their carers' mood state, there is, therefore, a good chance that you are more anxious generally than you might have been with more experienced, calmer parents.

Another important aspect in your upbringing is that, because you started life almost exclusively in the company of adults, you may set yourself very high standards and expectations. That's because we tend to measure ourselves in terms of those people we're around most often, and you compared yourself to individuals who were already far more capable than you were. Those high standards encourage high achievement, but they also mean you are often disappointed in your achievements because you tend to set such high expectations for yourself.

Adult first-borns tend to be keen to please those in authority (such people are in effect parental figures, after all), to be law-abiding and respectful of existing rules, to strive for and enjoy positions of leadership, to be organised, responsible, and academically successful, and to find it easy to be nurturing and caring. At the same time, you will tend to be highly self-critical and often anxious – and more likely to seek psychological help from professionals, (parental figures) when you feel overwhelmed.

Some examples of famous first-borns are Oprah Winfrey, Richard Branson and J.K. Rowling.

Middle-borns

If you're a middle-born, you'll have learned how to share and to get along with others right from birth. Because your parents were more experienced when you were born than they were when your older sibling came into the world, you're also likely to be more easy-going and relaxed than he or she is. Of course you, like your older sibling or any other child for that matter, wanted to do something particularly well so you would appear important and special to your parents. If, however, you had tried to gain your parents' admiration in the same way that your older sibling did, say by doing well in school, then you'd have difficulty outdoing an older sibling, who after all will always be more mature and developed than you are, simply through age. Therefore, you're more likely to choose something other than academics in which to pour your efforts, for example sports or music.

As an adult, you are usually able to get on with most people. After all, you were very often in a position of negotiation and compromise with others when you were a child, so you've had lots of practice – and no doubt you'll be good at it. Therefore later, when choosing a career, you'll be well able to work as part of a team – in fact, you may not feel particularly comfortable working on your own.

There is, however, a down side for someone who is always seeking compromise and trying to restore social harmony, and that is that you're probably easily led astray by others, and quite likely to give in to peer pressure even when group decisions go against your better judgment.

Because you grew up surrounded by peers, some a bit older and more capable than you and others younger and less mature, your models for setting your own standards will have been based as much on peers as it was on adults. That means you're likely to have more realistic expectations for yourself than will your older sibling.

Middle-borns are the ones in the family who are most likely to take up 'causes' and to support the needs of the downtrodden. This may be because you almost certainly had fewer opportunities to have special time and attention from your parents, and therefore may have felt lost or left out at times when you were growing up. When that happens we sometimes 'project' our own feelings about being left out or downtrodden onto others. Your crusades for the underprivileged may be a way of saying, 'We all deserve equal treatment. No one should be overlooked or left out.' This desire to help those whose needs are greater than your own may be reflected in your choice of career.

No doubt for similar reasons – that is, feeling over-looked when you were growing up – middle-borns often go through a phase of dressing bizarrely, sporting extreme hairstyles, or wearing unusual makeup. This is particularly true during the teenage years when all children are trying to carve out their individual identity. You are also very often the first child in the family to leave home, or at least you'll leave home at the youngest age.

The downside for middle-borns is that you are frequently plagued by a lack of direction in life. Perhaps this is because you have become so accustomed to downplaying your own dreams and desires in the interest of compromise and social harmony that, after a time, you lose awareness of them. It may also be that when you were young you deliberately hid your most heartfelt dreams and desires, and after a time of repressing your wishes repeatedly, they may have been pushed out of your conscious mind so you were no longer aware of them.

It's important to bear in mind that 'middle-born' is the least clearly defined birth order position. For example, are there character differences between middle-borns who are one of three children as opposed to one of say, seven? I've found that what tends to happen in larger families is that, although middle-borns all share many characteristics regardless of family size, smaller sibling 'sub-groups' often form, with some prominent first-born, middle-born and youngest child characteristics evident in those subgroups. This will be determined to a large extent by gender and age gap between siblings. So, for example, if you are the middle of three boys, you're likely to show strong middle-born characteristics. If, however, you are a middle-born but the only girl, then your profile will show a mixture of middle-born qualities and those attributed to first-borns (as the first girl in your family). If you're a middle-born and there's a large age gap between you and your next sibling, your profile will contain many last-born characteristics in addition to your middle child qualities.

Examples of famous middle-borns are Princess Diana, Stella McCartney and Bill Gates.

Last-borns

If you're the youngest, you're likely to be outgoing and charming – the entertainer or clown when you're around others. You're also more likely than those in other birth positions to be rebellious and to take risks. At the same time, you probably find it more difficult than others to organise your life efficiently, or to persist when the way ahead becomes difficult. Again, it's easy to see why.

As a child, you were the least mature and the least capable member of your family. Everyone around you appeared to you to be more able, so there was little chance you could outshine anyone and gain praise and attention as a result. Therefore, you learned to gain your attention by playing on your 'baby' qualities, by being cute, charming and seemingly helpless. Furthermore, if your parents had decided you were to be their last child, they may have inadvertently encouraged such immature behaviour because they saw you as their 'baby'. 'Charming' and 'entertaining' are positive attributes; however, if taken to extremes, you may become manipulative. As an adult, you're the one who's most likely to challenge authority and to be rebellious.

Your parents probably gave you more latitude than they gave to any of your siblings because they were more relaxed in their role than they were with your siblings. As a consequence you had to become more rebellious and take greater risks when you wanted to know what the limits in your family really were. Therefore, last-borns tend to be the risk takers.

Last-borns are also often highly creative. It's a fact that many of our greatest innovators and groundbreakers have been last-borns, or at least the youngest son or daughter in a family. This tendency to break new ground is also because, as a last-born, you wouldn't have had as many ways open to you when it came to attracting parental attention, because your older siblings will already have become competent in most, if not all, of the more conventional areas of achievement. Therefore, you naturally tend to be creative and to seek out new, less conventional ways of expressing yourself.

A large problem for last-borns is that you are vulnerable to low self-esteem and feelings of inferiority. Again, this makes sense when considering the circumstances in which you grew up. As a child, everyone around is bigger, stronger and more competent than you are. This is also true of first-borns, who start life surrounded by adults. However, after a time there's a new addition to the first-born's family, someone who's less able than the older child. The same never happens for you. As a result, you often feel inferior to others. Furthermore, as an adult you are often easily disappointed and prone to feeling 'let down' by others. This is because you probably grew up with the expectation that other people – particularly parental figures – will automatically 'know' what you want and that they'll generally be keen to provide it for you. Unfortunately for you, that's less often the case once you become an adult.

Examples of famous last-borns include Johnny Depp Joan of Arc and Eddie Murphy.

Single or 'only' children

Of all birth order positions, that of the single child has undergone the greatest transformation in recent years. Whereas it was once unusual – and in some communities, it was even considered unacceptable – to choose to have only one child, it's now very often a positive choice to have just the one. As the only child, you enjoy all the parental attention and input of a first-born, but without the resulting feelings of jealousy when you lose them. Furthermore, because one-child families are now much more common than they once were, it's meant that a number of the negative qualities associated with being the only child in a family, such as feeling isolated, or awkward when trying to socialise with peers, are no longer inevitably associated with being the only child. This is particularly true because nowadays parents are generally more aware of the needs of a growing child, and in particular of how important it is that a child learns good social skills. As a result, most go to great lengths to ensure that their child spends time with peers. Consequently, terms such as 'lonely' or 'socially isolated' no longer apply to most single children.

As the only child, you'll have enjoyed undivided attention from your carers, without ever having to know the jealousy that arises when you have to share that attention with other children. You'll have had lots of rich language input and are therefore likely to be articulate and to do well academically. You're also likely to be highly self-confident, to find it easy to spend time on your own, and to relate well to those who are older than you. As an adult, positions of responsibility and leadership come easily to you. On the other hand, you're also content to work on your own. You're most likely, too, to choose a more conventional career path.

You're also likely to be organised, logical and rational – in other words, more like the adults who surrounded you when you were growing up. However, that logical and ordered world can have a downside: single children often find it difficult to tolerate disorder. After all, you never had to get used to siblings who demanded attention at the same time you needed help, or to figure out how to deal with others who knocked over your toys or who in other ways created chaos in the house. That may mean that, as an adult, you appear impatient or demanding when things don't go according to plan. You may feel extremely uncomfortable, too, when things seems to be out of control, even when you know that this is only a temporary phenomenon.

Examples of famous first-borns are Leonardo da Vinci, Franklin Roosevelt, and Tiger Woods.

Other birth order effects

Birth order position isn't a simple 'formula'. All sorts of factors act on us as we grow up, modifying and softening some of our birth order characteristics, strengthening others, and sometimes creating qualities more remin- iscent of other birth order positions than the one we actually inhabit. Here are five of the most powerful 'sibling effects'.

1. *Multiple births in the family*

   If you're a twin or one of triplets, you'll probably have received lots of adult attention. Everyone is fascinated by multiple births, particularly when the children are identical, and the children are often treated as a single unit, dressed alike and often referred to as 'the twins'.

   However, the last thing a child wants is to have their individuality overlooked! More than anything, children want to be special and unique in their parents' eyes. Therefore, the more that twins or triplets are treated alike, the more each one will try to distinguish him or herself from the other(s). Although twins will inevitably share a close bond because they have so much shared experience, they'll also be highly competitive with one another. This competitiveness is so powerful that it may swamp any other birth order characteristics.

   The other factor when there's a multiple birth in the family is the effect this has on the other children, if there are others. I'm sure you've noticed how people stop and lavish attention on twins and triplets, and often while the other children must wait and watch patiently, virtually unnoticed. As a consequence, the others may be prone to feelings of low self-esteem, or on the other hand, feel driven to over-achieve in an attempt to attract the attention and praise they feel they deserved but didn't get. They may find it difficult to control feelings of jealousy throughout their lives, particularly when others are praised in their presence.

2. *When there are siblings who have special needs*
   When one child in the family has a disability, they will of course require extra attention. This will have a powerful effect on other children in the family. The others are quite likely to become good at nurturing and caring for others, and to take on positions of responsibility – in other words, to appear to be like first-borns. At the same time, they may grow up to champion the causes of the less fortunate – a middle-born quality.

   Children who have special needs may take on many of the qualities of a last-born, whatever their birth order position, because they must expect to be looked after and cared for. If they have a physical disability, knowing they'll have to struggle to live a 'normal' life may empower them, and they will grow up determined to be independent and 'make it' on their own, so in some ways they will resemble a single child. If their disability is all-pervasive – for example, if they're autistic – then their personality will be more determined by their disability than their birth order position.

3. *When a sibling dies*
   The death of a sibling has a profound and lasting effect on the entire family. After the initial grief and misery, it's natural to start thinking of the happier times that were spent with the child who has died, and to dwell on his or her best qualities, while often overlooking their faults. When a parent does this after the loss of a child, it can have an unfortunate effect on the other children.

They may begin to feel that they have little hope of emulating someone who, in the parents' eyes, becomes more and more perfect with the passage of time. As a result, they may suffer from low self-esteem, or become more prone to depression. On the other hand, they may set themselves impossibly high standards, and even if they achieve them, feel they're still not good enough.

4. *When step-siblings are introduced: the blended family*
Introducing more children into a family is a difficult challenge at the best of times. When several are introduced at once, and when they already occupy established positions within their original family, the competition for parental attention becomes intense. The qualities each child has developed as a consequence of his or her birth order position is, however, unlikely to change substantially unless the child is very young. That's because we establish the foundations of our identity between the ages of about three and six. Therefore, a child who suddenly finds him or herself in a 'new' birth order position will not suddenly lose the characteristics that have been forming for years.

What is likely, on the other hand, is that competition between children in the same respective birth positions – the first-borns, in each family, for example – will be intense and unpleasant for a time. This will be particularly so for first-borns, who have already lost parental attention once in their lives, and last-borns, who are used to being the centre of attention. Middle-borns will accommodate the new situation most easily. Whether the effect is lasting, and whether it is negative or beneficial, will depend almost entirely on how the parents of this new blended family handle the settling down period. If the parents present a united front, if they back each other up with regard to discipline, and if each child is praised for his or her unique talents and contribution to the new family, the overall effect in the long run will be that all the children will show increased tolerance towards others and an increased ability to cope with change.

5. *When a sibling comes back home to live: the boomerang child*
   Last but by no means least, what happens when a child who has grown up and left home then decides to return? This is determined to some extent by the reasons why the child has returned, and the conditions under which he or she is welcomed back.

   If the return is seen from the outset as temporary – perhaps the child had been travelling, and on return must wait to start a university course – then the return is usually welcomed by all. However, if the elder child has failed in some way – been made redundant, or perhaps was unable to meet mortgage repayments – then his or her distress will affect the rest of the family. Everyone may feel anxious, and worried about saying the 'wrong thing'. If parents dote on the returning child the other siblings, who have no doubt grown accustomed to the new arrangement and the extra attention and privileges they'd come to enjoy, may feel jealous and angry. The situation is unlikely to affect birth order characteristics, but everyone may become more anxious. The outcome for everyone depends crucially on how parents deal with the situation. If they treat the returning child no longer as a child, but instead as an adult, there will be less rivalry. This will also empower the returning child, particularly if he or she feels a failure in some way. Clarity is also important, particularly to minimise anxiety and jealous feelings in the other children. For example, how long the returning child expects to stay, and under what conditions, should be established and made clear to everyone.

As you can see, your family – in particular your parents' attitudes to you and to the world around them, as well as your position in the family relative to your siblings – will have had a profound effect on the development of your character.

There are other factors as well, of course – for example, how often you moved home, whether your parents divorced and if so whether they remarried, whether there were grandparents and other adults who played an important part in your family life, what the schools were like that you attended, and – particularly during your teenage years – what your friends were like and what you did together. None of these other factors is, however, as powerful as the effect your immediate family had on your character development.

No doubt you can now see how important it is to understand the relative contributions that your genetics and your experience have made on your character. Fundamentally, this helps you to know what aspects of your character you can change, and which aspects it's best that you work with to help you get the most out of your life. You now know that the greater part of your character is not innate, but that instead you learned to behave as you do in response to your environment when you were growing up. Therefore, if you wish to do so, you can override the habits that cause you distress, primarily by learning to respond in new, more fulfilling and adaptive ways.

How to Understand Your Character

1. Recognise the difference between those characteristics that are primarily genetic, and those that were formed because of an interaction between genetic makeup and early experience.

2. The two characteristics that are most heavily genetic are: how introverted or extroverted you are, and how impulsive or reflective. It's best to accept and work with these two dimensions. Consider how you can do so with regard to your relationships, your work and the best ways to look after yourself.

3. All other dimensions of your personality are based on a more equal contribution from your genetic makeup and your early experience. Therefore if you wish to do so, you can change many of the ways you behave and the attitudes you hold. However, take care! Consider change only if you desire it for yourself. If your motivation is rooted in a need to please others, it's far wiser to accept yourself as you are and capitalise on your strengths.

YOUR INTELLIGENCE PROFILE: WHAT KIND OF SMART ARE YOU?

The traditional concept of intelligence is, I hope, defunct. The idea that we can determine someone's general competence by asking him or her a limited series of short answer questions in an artificial environment and under strict time constraints, and then by reducing those answers to a single number (an IQ score), I consider to be outdated and limiting.

A much more helpful way to think about intelligence is to use the American developmental psychologist Howard Gardner's notion of multiple intelligences. In his book *Frames of Mind,* Gardner proposes six main types of intelligence (see References at page 255). This richer and more detailed picture of intellectual ability will allow you to discover your strengths and weaknesses, help you to choose interests that will give you the most satisfaction and pleasure, and guide you so you choose careers in which you're most likely to excel.

To discover your intelligence profile – that is, which types of intelligence are your strengths and which are weaker – you could download a wide variety of intelligence tests and test yourself, or you could pay to have a comprehensive intellectual or career assessment. However, Howard Gardner has a better suggestion – one that avoids any expense, one that means you won't be limited by a small number of standardised questions, and one that embodies the essence of *The Key to Calm*.

Gardner believes that it's possible to identify an individual's strengths and weaknesses simply by observing him or her repeatedly as they go about their daily lives. You can do this easily – in fact, I hope you've already started doing so – by being mindful on a frequent and regular basis. Become aware of which skills and types of thinking come most easily to you, and which ones represent more of a challenge. Become aware, too, of which activities you most often choose to do and which you most enjoy.

How to identify your strengths and weaknesses

The best way to discover your true intelligence profile is to think carefully and objectively about what areas of study you've always found easiest to understand and which ones you enjoy most, *whether you excelled in them in school or not*. Your school performance may have been affected by a number of factors that had little to do with your natural ability – poor teaching, or feeling ostracised and unhappy, for example. Your own reaction to the descriptions that you're about to read, as well as how you remember yourself as a child, will be a far more valuable guide than any school grades or test scores could ever be.

The six intelligences

Here, then, is a snapshot of each of the six abilities that Gardner identified. In addition to the description, I've suggested suitable careers associated with that intelligence, as well as some activities you might try to strengthen each one.

Linguistic intelligence

If you're linguistically smart, you will enjoy learning the meaning of individual words and understanding how language is put together. You'll be sensitive to and enjoy the rhythm and sounds of speech. You'll be keen to express yourself clearly, both in speaking and in writing. You're also likely to want to learn other languages.

You will almost certainly be an avid reader. You'll enjoy word games – Scrabble or crossword puzzles, for example – and 'playing' with language generally, for example by using puns. You will probably keep, or have kept, a diary or journal.

As a child, you loved to listen to stories and to be read to, to sing nursery rhymes, and perhaps to listen to and recite poetry. You loved acting in plays, perhaps even writing dramas yourself. You probably dreamed up lots of stories as well.

Best career choices

The ability to use language well and to communicate clearly and precisely, is of course an asset in almost any career. You're likely to do particularly well in those that emphasise speaking and conveying information – for example teaching, journalism and the law. If you are linguistically smart, you would do particularly well as a writer or poet, an editor, a linguist, or an actor.

How to strengthen linguistic intelligence

The easiest and most obvious way is to read more often and more widely. However, establishing a reading habit in today's 'sound bite' world isn't always easy. The best way to start is to set aside a manageable block of time – ten minutes is plenty. Make this at the same time of day (bed time is good, because the reading will help relax you in preparation for sleep). By making sure you read at the same time every day, the habit will become established more quickly. It doesn't matter what you choose to read, just choose something that really interests you.

You might also try doing some writing as well, or have a go at some crossword puzzles, code words or word scrambles. Perhaps see if you can find someone who will play a game of Scrabble with you. You might even consider learning new words, or another language.

One of my clients became more confident linguistically by learning a new word every week. She then set herself the challenge of using the word at least once each day in conversation.

Musical intelligence

The musically smart are sensitive to pitch and rhythm. You're likely to enjoy playing around with patterns of sound, arranging and rearranging bits of songs or passages of music.

Musical intelligence is the earliest of the six intelligence types to emerge. If you are musically intelligent, then as a baby you showed obvious delight when music was played, and as a child you probably spent a great deal of time listening to and creating rhythms. No doubt you were sensitive to changes in sounds in your environment. A xylophone, drum or toy guitar was probably a favourite toy. You may also have shown a particular interest in the sounds that different animals make.

Best career choices

Musical intelligence is of two main types. These are: the enjoyment of and desire to create music (composer), and the desire to perform music (instrumentalist or singer).

If you're musically intelligent, you would of course be well placed as a musician or singer, or as a composer if creating music was your predilection. However, musical intelligence also expresses itself in other areas. For example, a biologist may study the sounds that various animals make, and a dancer bases movement on rhythm. If linguistic intelligence is another strength, you'd make a good broadcaster, or perhaps a lyricist.

How to strengthen musical intelligence

The obvious suggestion is to take voice lessons or learn to play a musical instrument. When you listen to music see if you can identify the various instruments used, or the type of rhythm. Simply listening mindfully to a wide variety of music is probably the best, easiest and most enjoyable way to strengthen musical intelligence.

Logico-mathematical intelligence

If you're intelligent in this sphere, then maths and science are your realms. You search for generalisations: if this is true in one case, will it be true in other situations? Note, however, that your powerful desire to understand the rules and laws that govern the physical world, to think about symbols even more than the reality they symbolise, may mean that you appear 'remote' or less sociable when you're with other people.

Individuals who possess strong logico-mathematical intelligence will enjoy conducting experiments, whether as a hobby or by choosing a career that demands experimentation. They'll also be keen to practise mindfulness, although it will be difficult for them merely to observe, without trying to explain and predict!

As a young child, you loved to order and re-order objects, and to count things. Later on, you were keen to understand the laws that relate one object or sphere of activity to another. Science and maths were no doubt favourite subjects.

Best career choices

If this describes you, good career choices are any in which mathematics and the sciences predominate. Research – either as an academic subject or in research and development in industrial settings – would be an excellent choice. You'd make a good accountant or engineer. If you also love words, then philosophy and logic are the subjects for you.

How to strengthen logico-mathematical intelligence

Put the calculator away! Try your hand at arithmetic whenever possible. One of my patients, who was determined to overcome her fear of venturing out into public places, created a distraction technique that had the pleasing side effect of improving her confidence in her arithmetical skills and her ability to budget. Before she went out to the shops she would set a limit on the amount she could spend on groceries. As she went down the aisles of the shop, rather than worrying about the other people around her, she looked for the price of each item she wanted to buy and added it to her tally, always making sure she kept within her budget.

Another way to strengthen mathematical intelligence is to consider learning more about a particular branch of maths or science. If you do so, be sure to choose a teacher you feel can make things clear to you. There are many individuals who are actually quite logical and mathematically smart, but who gave up learning early on because they were badly taught. This intelligence, more than any other, is systematic. That means that if you didn't learn an early step, you'll have felt lost from that time on. Go back to basics, and you may discover a hidden talent.

Spatial intelligence

If you're spatially intelligent you will be able to appreciate how things move through space in relation to one another. You'll find it easy, for example, to recognise that one object is the same as another, but that it's shown at a different angle or in a different rotation. You'll be very good at pattern recognition.

You will also be able easily to find your way between two locales. You enjoy reading maps and you rarely get lost.

As a child you loved treasure hunts, exploring and getting around in new places generally. You also enjoyed toys that create patterns or with which you can make structures – stick-on shapes, Lego™ or Meccano™, for example.

Best career choices

If you're spatially smart you'd do well as a scientist, particularly as a physicist or astrophysicist. You'd also make a good architect, landscape architect, interior designer or sculptor. If logical-mathematical intelligence is another strength, you'd make a good surgeon. My husband has great difficulties with mathematics, but is extremely artistic and has excellent spatial skills. A career as an architect has suited him well.

How to strengthen spatial intelligence

Visit new places and use a map to find your way around. You might also try to make a map of the locations you visit. Look for puzzles and games that require you to identify the same object as it is seen at different angles. If you love the outdoors and can afford it, take a course in garden design.

Bodily-kinaesthetic intelligence

If you possess this sort of intelligence then you, like the spatially intelligent, will be interested in the movement of objects through space. However, your interest will be primarily in how you can manipulate those objects yourself to make them move, or how you can move about most effectively and efficiently yourself.

You're likely to be athletic and enjoy gaining mastery over the motion of your own body. Whether you choose to compete as an athlete has more to do with your personality – that is, whether or not you're competitive – than whether you possess bodily-kinaesthetic intelligence. However, if you're smart in this way, you'll love movement and you'll take every opportunity to gain new physical skills.

As a child, you loved throwing and catching, pushing objects up and down slopes, dancing, playing sports, and generally being physically active. No doubt you had a go at most physical activities, but you were – and probably still are – particularly keen on the all-body sports such as swimming, running, cycling and dancing. Ball games are likely to be a passion.

Best career choices
Any work that involves lots of moving around, as well as a high level of physical fitness, is for you. You'd make a great sportsman of course. The military and the police force are other possibilities. You'd make an excellent osteopath or chiropractor if logico-mathematical and spatial intelligence are also your stronger points. Acting is another possibility

One child I was asked to assess showed extremely high logico-mathematical, bodily-kinesthetic and spatial skills, but was failing at school. He told me that sport, particularly strength training and practical 'hands on' work, was his passion. He knew he could do the academic work, but the interest just wasn't there. He later chose to become a car mechanic and has excelled in his trade.

How to strengthen bodily-kinaesthetic intelligence
Taking up any new sport will help you, but check with your doctor first if you've not been active for some time, and find a good instructor. Learning yoga, or Pilates, or taking up the Alexander Technique (a one-to-one teaching programme that emphasises best positioning of the body) would be helpful as well, because these activities help you balance your body and strengthen any weak areas.

Personal intelligence

If you have personal intelligence, you're a people watcher. First and foremost, you'll have an enduring interest in and ability to assess your own emotional state – how you're feeling and thinking and why.

You'll be interested in and keen to notice what other people are doing and saying, and in trying to figure out why they're behaving as they are. You'll also enjoy making distinctions among people, and trying to determine their motives.

You may also enjoy drawing, characterising or taking photographs of people.

As a child, you loved stories. However, unlike the child whose linguistic intelligence is strongest, you preferred stories that someone told you about themselves – in particular, their own adventures and early experiences. You also loved to imagine and make up stories about people. Dressing up was no doubt a favourite activity, particularly if bodily-kinaesthetic intelligence is another of your strengths.

Best career choices

If you possess personal intelligence, you'd make a good photographer or artist – if, that is, you also possess good spatial and bodily-kinaesthetic intelligence. You'd also make a good psychologist, doctor, social worker, teacher or actor. If your other strengths include logico-mathematical and spatial intelligence, you'd make a good detective. If they include logico-mathematical and linguistic intelligence, you'd be a good GP.

How to strengthen personal intelligence
Practise listening mindfully to what other people tell you. Ask lots of questions. When you first meet someone, see if you can guess what sort of job they have, and what their interests might be. Take a course in portraiture or life drawing, or sign up for an introductory psychology course.

Creating your own intelligence profile

Now that you've read through these six descriptions, I hope you've found yourself several times at least. It's encouraging and great fun to read passages with which you can identify.

However, to look at each of the six intelligences in isolation is interesting, but it won't produce the most accurate profile. A better way to use what you've learned is to list your intelligences in order, from the strongest one to the weakest. Taken together, your two or three strongest intelligences will be your best guide when you look for a satisfying career.

Here's an example. Let's say that music is the intelligence you consider to be your strongest. If your second strongest is spatial intelligence then you'll be better at composing music than at playing it. If spatial and linguistic intelligences are your other two strong qualities, then you'd make a good lyricist. If on the other hand, spatial and bodily-kinaesthetic are your other strong intelligences, you're likely to be a good instrumentalist or singer.

Likewise if you love studying law. If your top two

intelligences are linguistic and logico-mathematical, you'd make a good solicitor. If on the other hand linguistic, logic-mathematical and bodily-kinaesthetic are all equally strong, you might consider becoming a barrister, because not only do you find that you can comprehend laws as represented through language, but you also probably enjoy putting yourself in a situation where you need to convince others of what you know.

If when choosing your career path you work with your strengths, you're most likely to choose careers in which you'll do well and truly enjoy. However, what should you do if you've already chosen a particular career path and invested time and training into it, only to find that it suits you less well than you'd imagined?

If you're truly unhappy, the boldest step would be to look for some sort of training scheme that would allow you to leave your current employment and retrain. One of my patients did just this. He was extremely unhappy as an accountant, primarily because the work was too solitary for him. He longed to be part of a lively social group at work and to work directly with people. He discovered a Government scheme that paid him to retrain as a teacher, and is now happily teaching mathematics in a secondary school.

An alternative course would be to find a better way, within your current employment to use your strengths. For example, another of my patients found himself unhappy working in IT in a large corporation. Our discussions made it clear that his strongest intelligences were logico-mathematical and personal. It was the latter he felt he was missing. He wanted, he told me, to solve people problems rather than computer problems. He decided to approach his manager at work for help. As a result, he was able to retrain within the company and is now enjoying a position in HR, still with his original company.

Finally, remember that to feel good about your life is to feel competent in a number of ways, rather than just one or two, so you'll also want to work on your weaker intelligences to equalise your profile. This is best done when it doesn't matter so much whether your performance or output is of the highest quality. Therefore, you'll feel most like challenging yourself in your leisure time. Consider having a go at some of the suggestions in the preceding sections.

By capitalising on your strengths, and at the same time becoming more able in areas where you're not so strong, you'll feel more balanced. Your self-esteem will grow and you'll feel calmer and more prepared to meet any new challenges you may encounter.

How to discover and use your intelligence profile

1. Discard the notion of IQ. This is merely an age-related comparison of what you learned at school and how well you were taught – it predicts little else.

2. Think instead in terms of a profile of intelligences. There are six of these to consider. Read the descriptions to

discover your strengths and identify your weaker abilities. It will help if you can recall your favourite activities when you were a child.

3. Rank in order the six intelligences to create your profile.

4. Use your top two or three intelligences to help you decide best career choices.

5. If you've already invested time and training in an area that you now realise isn't the one that optimises your greatest strengths, look for ways you could make better use of your talents within your current employment, perhaps by retraining within the organisation. If that's not possible, look for schemes that will fund you to retain in a more suitable area. You might also consider finding at least one new way to use your strengths and talents outside of work.

6. Consider ways to build up your weaker intelligences, so you can create a more balanced profile.

YOUR PASSIONS

I've saved the best for last.

When you understand your personality and know why you've come to be the way you are, you'll know which situations will bring out the best in you and the ones in which you must behave with greater caution and attention. When you chart your intelligences profile you'll discover your strengths and weaknesses, and that in turn will mean you can capitalise on your strengths where it's important that you perform at your best, and find ways to improve upon your weaknesses in relative safety.

However, when you discover – or in most cases, *re*discover – your passions, you'll get in touch with the energy that will make everything else in your life possible. It is when we realise our passions that we are most truly alive.

Knowing what it means to express yourself through your passions

The author and academic Mihaly Csikszentmihalyi describes eloquently how we feel when we're pursuing our passions. He calls this 'flow' or 'optimal experience', and he describes it thus:

> *'The best moments occur when a person's body or mind is stretched to its limits in a voluntary effort to accomplish something difficult and worthwhile. Optimal experience is thus something that we make happen. For a child, it could be placing with trembling fingers the last block on a tower she has built, higher than any she has built so far; for a swimmer, it could be trying to beat his own record; for a violinist, mastering an intricate musical passage.'*
>
> (*Flow*, p. 3)

At first glance, it can be easy to confuse passion with expressing your personality or using some aspect of your intelligence. It's not, however, the same thing. If you're striving to win a race, if your only aim is to beat everyone else, then you're demonstrating ambition – and that's a personality characteristic rather than a type of intelligence. Winning may make you feel satisfied, but you won't experience true joy. If you're running that race because you know you're good at it and easily capable of winning, you're expressing your bodily-kinaesthetic intelligence, and again, you'll feel satisfied with a job well done. However, you won't feel the same exhilaration you'd feel if you push yourself to your limits purely for the joy of doing so, never mind anyone else. Surprisingly, when you're in pursuit of your passions you often know discomfort, yet at the same time you'll feel most fully alive. Csikszentmihalyi again explains:

'Such experiences are not necessarily pleasant at the time they occur. The swimmer's muscles might have ached during his most memorable race, his lungs might have felt like exploding, and he might have been dizzy with fatigue – yet these could have been the best moments of his life. Getting control of life is never easy, and sometimes it can be definitely painful. But in the long run optimal experiences add up to a sense of mastery – or perhaps better, a sense of participation in determining the content of life – that comes as close as what is usually meant by happiness as anything else we can conceivably imagine.'

(*Flow*, pp. 3–4)

What allows *you* to experience flow? What pastimes do you return to, time and again, just because you *want* to? What were you doing when, suddenly, you realised that you'd lost all sense of time and hours have flown by? These are your passions.

Each of us will have a different array of passions just as each of us, like the snowflake, is unique. For me it's writing, swimming and dancing. For one of my children it's playing her drums. For another, it's tinkering with and repairing engines.

How to rediscover your passions

If you can't name a passion, then your life is starved of energy and is unbalanced. You probably feel overwhelmed by obligations, by a sense of 'should'. You no doubt feel exhausted much of the time. If that's the case, you'll benefit enormously from Step Four, when you will learn to take control of the 'shoulds' in your life and restore a balance that will allow you some much-needed time to enjoy your passions.

First, however, you need to rediscover what those passions are. Here are two ways that can help you:

Go back to middle childhood

My clients always enjoy this exercise.

Close your eyes and think back to when you were about nine or ten years old, the last two years at primary school. How did you spend your free time then? What were your main interests, your hobbies, the things you loved most to do?

If you can't remember much, see if you can find some old photographs or scrapbooks or, if you kept them, old diaries. These may awaken some memories.

If you can't find any such items, contact your siblings if you have any, or your parents or childhood friends, and ask them to describe what they remember about you. Reminiscing with relatives and well-established friends is therapeutic itself, as you'll learn in Step Five. Therefore, taking the time to contact people from your past will be rewarding, whatever they tell you. However, in addition to enjoying yourself, you're quite likely to learn things from these encounters. They're likely to resurrect memories you may have forgotten.

You may be wondering why I've suggested this particular age. The reason is that between the ages of about nine and eleven, what you did and cared about represents your true self more accurately than anything you did or cared about in the past, or are likely to ever again.

The reason why this age is so important in terms of self-discovery is that it's the period of time when you're least influenced by the demands of other people and by your need to please anyone else. This is because you were a baby, you were totally dependent on your carers to look after you, feed you, keep you warm, and in all other ways to nurture you. That meant that your entire focus was to please those carers. After all, if they loved you and considered you important, then they'd look after you. Therefore, what you did was to please them, much more so than to express your individuality.

As you grew into a toddler and then a young child, you began to do more and more for yourself, and to look after yourself. By the time you were about nine or ten, you could probably take care of many of your basic needs. That meant that you needed to devote less of your energy to making sure your parents were pleased with you, and you had more time to please yourself.

However, once adolescence kicked in, things changed again. At that point, your overwhelming desire was to belong, to be considered acceptable and popular with your peers. Once again, much of your energy was channelled into pleasing others – only this time, the 'others' were your peers.

I hope you can see, therefore, why the year or two before puberty is the time when you're most likely to be expressing your own unique talents, and pursuing your own passions. Once you've found memorabilia from this period in your past, and after you've contacted people from your childhood, take some time to consider what you've discovered. Can you modify or adapt any of your childhood passions, so that you can incorporate them into your life now?

If you can't do so, or if you weren't able to discover any passions, then try the following exercise:

Write morning pages

The artist and author Julia Cameron has written a wonderful book called *The Artist's Way* to help individuals reconnect with their creative self. In this book she suggests a technique that may well allow you to rediscover your passions. She calls this technique 'the morning pages'. I've adapted her suggestions for our purposes. Here's what you do:

Put a pen or pencil and a notebook by your bed when you settle down at night. Set your alarm for ten minutes earlier than usual.

When you wake, the first thing you'll do is to write down in the notebook *whatever is going through your mind at the time.* This may be the dream you were just dreaming. It might be thoughts about the coming day, or a memory from yesterday. It might be some distant memory that, for some unknown reason, is in your conscious mind. It doesn't matter what it is, or in what order it comes out. Just write it down. Do this for ten minutes. Then put the notebook away and begin the day proper with your five minutes of mindful awareness.

Do this for two weeks.

Cameron calls this exercise 'brain drain' (p. 10), because her main interest in suggesting it is to give the user a way to empty his or her mind of the 'rubbish' and the self-criticism that so often blocks artistic endeavour.

Our interest, however, is not so much in the emptying as in *what has been emptied.* Whereas Cameron asks her readers not to look at what they've written, I'll want you to do just the opposite. Please do look at what you've written. You can read it as you go along, or every few days, or you can wait and read everything you've written at the end of the two weeks. It doesn't matter.

The purpose of this exercise is to allow you to get in

touch with many of the thoughts, desires and dreams that normally would be pushed out of your conscious mind by the demands of a busy day. The material you've allowed yourself to access may well offer you the clues you need to rediscover your passions.

The next step

Now that you're aware of ways to experience flow again, you'll want to incorporate them into your life as soon as possible. Allowing yourself time to do what you love doing is far from selfish, by the way! When you factor into your schedule regular spaces of time to express yourself, you'll notice an increase in your energy levels generally. As a result, you'll find it easier to do everything else you need to do.

Becoming mindful (Step One) and incorporating times to express your unique self (this Step Three) are the two most important aspects of *The Key to Calm*. They, more than anything else you do, will allow you to regain and maintain a sense of balance and fulfilment in your life.

How to Rediscover Your Passions

1. To rediscover your passions is to rediscover the source of your creative energy.

2. Think back to when you were nine or ten years old, just before puberty. What were your interests and

enthusiasms at that time? How might you adapt them to become part of your life today?

3. If you can't remember that time well, try putting a notebook and pen by your bed. Immediately upon waking each morning, write down whatever is passing through your mind, in the order it presents itself to you. This can help you to recall interests and enthusiasms you've lost touch with as your life became overwhelmed with duties and obligations.

4. Consider the interests and enthusiasms you've rediscovered to be every bit as important as anything else you do now. Find ways to make them part of your life once more.

Step Four:
Streamline Your Life

'*Our life is frittered away by detail.*
Simplify, simplify.'
Henry David Thoreau

We all have too much clutter in our lives.

There's the psychological clutter, the obligations and 'shoulds' in your life. They make you feel tired and resentful rather than more fulfilled or more balanced. Then there's the physical clutter, the clothes you never wear, the collections of this and that you promise yourself you'll sort someday. These get in your way and prevent you seeing ahead clearly. Finally, there's the procedural clutter, the emails you answer immediately when they're not a priority, the committees you've volunteered to serve on but that you don't really have time for. All these things keep you busy, but not in the ways you really want to be. That's why, whenever someone suggests that you try something new and interesting, you feel conflicted, maybe even irritated. Here's something really tempting, you think. How I'd love to try that!

However, when you look at your diary, no doubt your heart sinks. How will it be possible to add *anything* to your timetable when a major source of stress in your life is the fact that you have too much to do already?

In this chapter you'll learn how to find the space in your schedule that you so badly need. We'll begin by clearing out the clutter that gets in the way of effective, satisfying living. You'll then learn how to plan effectively and realistically. Finally, I'll explain how you can protect the spaces you've created in your schedule by saying 'no' in ways that show you really mean it.

DECLUTTER PSYCHOLOGICALLY

When I meet with clients for the first time, I listen as carefully to *how* they talk about their lives as I do to *what* their schedules entail. By doing this, I seldom need to ask them to identify the circumstances in which they feel particularly stressed. That's because when you describe your daily life, the sense of control you feel will be revealed in the words you choose. That sense of control, rather than the number of things you have to do, is the key to reducing the amount of stress you're feeling.

Therefore, the first step to reducing stress is to become aware of how you describe your daily activities. For example, if your language is peppered with phrases like 'I have to', 'I should', and 'I really don't believe I have any choice', then it's a sure bet that you're feeling anxious, stressed and out of control. Although all these phrases are noteworthy, for our purposes the most powerfully revealing is the phrase 'I should'.

Whenever you start talking about a 'should' – 'I really *should* go the gym more often', or 'I really *should* try for a promotion' – then you can be sure you've identified a 'hot' area, an issue about which you feel conflicted and stressed. The reason for this is that the word 'should' implies an obligation, a sense of duty arising out of your need or desire to please someone *other than yourself*. When you say 'should', you're intimating that you're trying to live up to an ideal that someone else has established for you, rather than that you're making a decision based on your own talents and passions. 'Should' means 'I don't really want to do this. I'm just trying to please.'

Let's consider the two examples above. If you say, 'I really love going to the gym', then working out in the gym is a good way for you to stay fit. You've chosen to do it, and by and large you enjoy the experience. If on the other hand you say, 'I really should go to the gym', then it's almost certain that you don't enjoy working out there. You joined the gym perhaps because a friend who's really fit belongs to that gym, or because you thought that if you can tell everyone you belong to a gym they'll be more impressed with you. As a result, you're wasting precious moments of your life every time you go to the gym.

Furthermore, because you have to force yourself to exercise when you're there, you derive less benefit from that workout than you would if you were to do something you'd describe as 'good fun' – for example, spending an hour in the garden or taking a walk with a friend.

Similarly, if you say, 'I really should try for a promotion', you're probably feeling that obligation because you want to show your parents or your partner or someone else you care about that you're more go-ahead than they thought. Or perhaps you're afraid of appearing lazy compared to your colleagues, so you claim to want a promotion when in fact you're perfectly happy doing the job you're doing now.

If on the other hand you say, 'I'd really love to be promoted', then you probably will be. You no doubt know what position you want to be promoted to, you've made it your business to know what you need to do so you'll be given that promotion, and you'll have the energy to do whatever is needed to gain you that promotion.

When you allow yourself to be directed by the 'shoulds' in your life, you'll feel less motivated than if you do what *you* believe is right and best. You'll also be more anxious than you would be if your enthusiasms and talents were your guides, rather than other people's assertions about what's right for you.

If your habit is always to look to others for direction and approval, that means you have to be ever watchful, constantly trying to gauge other people's reactions about what you're doing. You'll rarely, if ever, experience the joy of being in 'flow' because 'flow' is fully absorbing – there's no space left to be searching about for approval. You'll also find it difficult to plan ahead because you're always poised to change your plans if you sense that what you're doing doesn't meet with approval from someone whose opinions you consider more important than your own.

Clearing away the sense of obligation

Most 'shoulds' are so automatic that, most of the time, you probably don't even notice their existence. Therefore, the first step when you declutter psychologically is to become aware of the messages that stop you feeling in charge of your life direction. This is where mindfulness comes in, and why it was so important that you started on the path to calm by learning to be mindful. During one of your mindfulness sessions each day, listen to your 'inner chatter' and listen out in particular for those tell-tale 'shoulds'.

There are other ways to become aware of the 'shoulds' that are robbing you of a sense of control. For example, listen to the way you describe your daily activities when you're speaking with others. Another good way to do this is to ask your partner or a colleague or friend to point out the times when you talk about what you 'should' do. You'll no doubt be surprised to find how often this occurs!

It doesn't matter whether you're telling yourself what's next on your agenda, or whether you're explaining your actions to someone else. Just start noticing whenever you hear that word 'should'. Whenever it appears, ask yourself the following three questions:

1. Why 'should' I do this? What do I think I'll get out of doing it? Who do I imagine I'm pleasing when I comment that I 'should' do whatever it is?
2. What would happen if I didn't do whatever I said I 'should' do? Is this action truly necessary, or am I doing it simply to gain approval from someone other than myself?
3. If the action is necessary, is there any way I could achieve a similar outcome, but do so in a way that I would enjoy more?

The answer to the first question will allow you to become aware of when you act out of obligation rather than choice. You then need to ask yourself why you feel the need to be dictated to by this person, and why now? Perhaps once upon a time it made sense to try to please him or her, but is that still the case?

The truth is, however obvious it sounds, you're more likely to feel happy and balanced in your life if you work from your own strengths and passions, rather than if you feel driven to please other people.

Your answer to the second question will help you decide whether to discard this sense of obligation altogether, or whether you can proceed, and answer the third question. In other words, if you do still need to carry out an obligation, can you do so in a way that energises and motivates you – so that it is something you really *want* to do? It's always possible to turn an obligation into an enthusiasm.

A Case Study

One of my clients, James, is a nurse in the local hospital. He'd made an appointment to see his GP because he felt too stressed and exhausted to get to work. His GP could find nothing wrong physically and concluded that James was suffering from stress. He therefore suggested that James made an appointment to see me.

James began by telling me that he enjoyed his work as a nurse, but that at the same time he'd always felt uncomfortable in busy social settings – which most hospitals are. Therefore, he'd had to search quite carefully before he could find a job that suited him. He felt he'd found the right situation by working night shifts in a surgical ward, and for several years this had worked well.

Recently, however, a more senior position had become vacant in the hospital and his line manager had suggested that he apply. The problem for James was that this was a day job, so he knew it would therefore demand far more social interaction. He felt under severe pressure to apply for the job, but at the same time he felt certain that he wouldn't be able to cope with the increased social pressures. He'd begun to feel paralysed and confused, unable to sleep or to make decisions.

When I asked him why he felt the need to apply for the job he said that he felt it was wrong to pass up a chance for promotion, that he 'really *should* seize every chance to earn more money', and that he 'should be able to cope in busy social environments'.

When we began to unravel his 'shoulds', James realised that he was allowing his past to dictate the present. He explained that he felt his parents had always preferred his older brother to him. This brother was sociable, extroverted, extremely ambitious, and he enjoyed a high-paying job. His parents valued such qualities enormously so, as a consequence, when the two brothers were young, James' parents had frequently made unfavourable comparisons between him and his brother. As a result, James had come to feel that he 'should' be more like his brother.

Once I explained that introversion was a natural and enduring part of his character, something that had been a part of him since birth rather than some sort of bad habit he'd learned, James began to relax. He was able to recognise that the source of his internal conflict was an automatic, unconscious habit that was firmly rooted in the past and was of no help now.

James then decided that there was no need to give up what he enjoyed doing now, simply because he 'should'. He willingly accepted that there was nothing wrong with being introverted and recognised that others, mainly his brother, might gain great satisfaction by socialising frequently and setting very high targets for themselves. However, this would only make a person happy, James reasoned, if the personality matched the effort required, and for him it did not. James was then able to accept that there was no need – no 'should' – to apply for a promotion he would not enjoy. After this understanding his distressing symptoms began to disappear.

What happens when you clear away the 'shoulds'

Many of my clients are at first reluctant to let go of their 'shoulds'. Many worry that if they don't push themselves, they'll become totally undirected and lazy, and that they'll never finish anything.

Nothing could be further from the truth!

Once you stop making yourself do things that are intended only to please other people, you'll feel a huge sense of relief. You'll also begin to notice that you have more energy, and that you can make decisions more quickly and with greater confidence.

Once you decide to do what *you* believe is the right thing to do, to do what *you* believe makes the best use of your passions, your intelligences and your talents, you'll start looking forward to each day. You'll find a sense of purpose that will see you through the tough times and that grants you the staying power necessary to overcome any obstacles that arise.

This will have nothing to do with ambition or career advancement, by the way. Say for example that you decide that, more than anything, you really want to spend more time at home. Perhaps you have young children and you want to be with them before they start school. You therefore resign from the prestigious job you now hold in a city some miles away, and instead you find a part-time job locally. If that decision comes from within *you,* rather than that it arises from a need to fulfil someone else's expectation of what you *should* do, I can assure you that you won't worry about what others will make of your decision.

Furthermore, even when what you're doing is compulsory, when it's a tiring obligation rather than a joy, you can still feel in charge of your life direction. The key is to focus on *why* you're doing whatever it is, rather than on *what* is involved. Even when there's little or no choice about what you do, it's always in your power to decide why you're doing it.

Let me show you what I mean.

Suppose you're spending many hours each week looking after your elderly mother. You find the tasks difficult and tiring and none of your siblings have offered to help. Because you believe you have no choice, you're resentful and exhausted most of the time. You've even started to find it difficult to drive to your mother's house, and you rarely enjoy the time you spend with her.

Let's say that you've decided to reassess your situation. You think that, instead of feeling obligated and helpless, you'll decide that you're helping your mum because you know it will make all the difference to her quality of life.

You're proud of your sense of values, of the importance you attach to family ties. You also realise that you're good at looking after other people, even though you don't necessarily love doing so. With such a change in perspective, your resentment and distress will diminish.

Once you see what you're doing as a choice rather than a burden, you'll feel better, even though what you're doing hasn't actually changed. Attitude can make any action seem good or bad. This has been recognised for centuries – to quote Shakespeare's *Hamlet*, 'There is nothing either good or bad, but thinking makes it so'. Furthermore, if in addition to this change in attitude you'll practise mindfulness when you're with your mum, you'll start to see and accept her as she is now, rather than as you wish she still could be.

Finally, there's yet another benefit when you discard all sense of obligation. You'll enjoy a sense of 'flow' more often. This is the feeling I described in Step Three, the feeling you get when you're fully engaged in the present moment and using your talents and abilities to their fullest extent. You can only know 'flow' when you're completely absorbed, when you aren't distracted by thoughts of how your choice may be perceived by other people. To experience 'flow' you must feel fully committed, doing what you believe to be right for you, regardless of what others think about you.

The 18th century philosopher Goethe offered one of the best explanations of what will happen when you trust your judgment and commit fully to doing what you believe to be right. I often give my clients a copy of his wise words:

'*Until one is committed there is the chance to draw back, always ineffectiveness.*

Concerning all acts of initiative (and creation) there is one elementary truth, the ignorance of which kills countless ideas and splendid plans.

That the moment one definitely commits oneself, then Providence moves too.

All sorts of things occur to help one that would not otherwise have occurred.

A whole stream of events issues from the decision, raising in one's favour all manner of unforeseen incidents and meetings and material assistance which no man could have dreamed would have come his way.

Whatever you do, or dream you can, begin it!

Boldness has genius, magic and power in it.

Begin it now!'

How to Declutter Psychologically

1. Become aware of the way you describe your daily life and, in particular, note the 'shoulds' in your speech. Use your ability to be mindful to help increase your awareness. You might also ask your partner or a friend

---

to point out the occasions when you speak in terms of 'should'.

2. Whenever you notice a 'should', ask yourself three questions:

   a) Why am I feeling this obligation? Who am I trying to please, and why do I feel the need to gain their approval?

   b) What would happen if I didn't do whatever it is? In other words, is it a truly necessary action, or am I merely doing it to gain the approval of someone other than myself? If it's the latter, consider not doing whatever it is.

   c) If I do need to carry out this action, is there any way I can achieve a similar outcome by doing so in a more enjoyable way, a way that feels more like the desire to do it is coming from within me?

Questions a) and b) will help you to decide whether you really do need to do anything that's a 'should'. If not, you needn't spend time on it.

If you feel it is important to act, use question c) to help you decide how to rephrase your intent so that you refer to whatever it is more in terms of a choice than an obligation. That in turn will motivate and energise you, and as a result you'll be more efficient and effective when you take action.

DECLUTTER PHYSICALLY

Do you have a wardrobe full of clothes, but in fact you only wear a small proportion of them? Is your house full of items you never use, but that you hold onto anyway 'just in case'? Is your workspace filled with papers you intend to sort, and emails you intend to answer, 'someday'?

If you have more than you need – and most of us in the West do – you'll feel overloaded and anxious. You'll find it difficult to focus your attention, have trouble making decisions, and you'll be less efficient when you finally get started. Perhaps most surprisingly is that in the long run you'll also feel less satisfied about your life than you'd feel if you had fewer possessions. The more you can simplify your living space and your workplace, the calmer and more contented you'll feel.

Let's take a look at what happens when you have a good deal more than you need.

More possessions imply more obligations

You may think that your material possessions offer you a sense of security and happiness. In fact, however, more often than not they represent a source of anxiety.

The more you own, and the more valuable are the things that you own, the more you have to worry about. You have to maintain what you own. You may have to insure it. You have to lock it up whenever you're parted from it. These considerations are costly and they create stress. There are other, more enjoyable ways to spend your time and energy!

Five traps that can clutter up your life

To avoid a life that's filled with physical clutter, make yourself aware of the five most common traps that encourage you to have too much:

The trap of confusing 'I need' with 'I want'

The overriding reason that you own more than is in your best interests is that you – like most of us – have come to believe that what you want is the same thing as what you need. It's not.

Your needs are quite simple: sufficient warmth, adequate food and shelter, and companionship at a level that feels comfortable for you. That's it. Everything else is a 'want' rather than a need.

That doesn't mean that you'll be happiest if you limit yourself to the basic necessities and nothing more! We all love a bit of luxury. However, if you keep the distinction in mind, and remember that almost everything you think you need is actually a luxury, then not only will you make more careful decisions, you'll also enjoy what you have far more, because you'll be more aware of your luxuries and privileges.

The trap of duplication

Another common trap you may fall into is the trap of duplication, of owning a number of different items that in fact all fulfil the same role. For example, one of my clients came to me complaining that he didn't have enough time to do the work demanded of him by his employer. It's true that he had a full schedule. However, this man had two paper diaries, one at work and one at home. He also had two electronic diaries, one for work and for home, and he backed both of them up on his computer. He also had a personal secretary who kept track of his work engagements, with whom he met each morning to run through those engagements. When I asked him to keep track of the amount of time he was spending recording and checking what he had to do, he was astonished to find that these activities took up over two hours of his time every day!

The trap of feeling that what you have is outdated, and because of that reason and only that reason, needs replacing

A third fallacy is the notion that, in order to perform at your best, you 'need' the most up-to-date version of whatever you already have, just as soon as the newer version becomes available. This is easily done, because we're all constantly pressured by advertisers who suggest we 'need' to be up to date with faster and faster ways of doing everything.

More often than not, however, the increased 'efficiency' we're offered resides only in the gadget! Slowing down a bit, and taking time to reflect on all possibilities before you act, will mean you make wiser decisions and fewer mistakes. It's well known that the faster you react, the greater is the chance that you'll have regrets. Just think about the number of times you wish you'd waited before replying to an email or a text!

In truth, upgrading before you really need to do so represents an unnecessary expense, and it's likely to make you less efficient, less accurate, and more stressed rather than better at what you do. Your state of mind is what counts, not the newness of the gadgets you own.

The trap of feeling unable to let go

It's a natural and normal tendency to accumulate possessions. We feel safer when we're surrounded by 'stuff'. The reason for this is that human beings are, relative to most other creatures, quite needy in our natural state. We need clothing and shelter to feel comfortable, and we need a wide selection of food to maintain best health. We also need other people to care for us when we're young, and this is so for quite a long time compared to most other creatures. So the feeling of being 'accompanied' or 'surrounded' is very basic.

The problem today, however, is that we in the West have easy access to too much. As a result, it's very easy to find that we've ended up with more than we need to feel safe – so much more, in fact, that we start to feel overburdened and overloaded, and therefore not safe at all. If you're feeling that way, your initial reaction will be to hold on to everything you have, to 'protect' yourself by surrounding yourself. As a result, you'll simply feel even more overburdened and out of control.

Another reason we feel the need to have so much is that we rarely encounter directly those who have too little. If we did, our inclination to reach out and look after others of our own kind – what scientists refer to as altruism – would encourage us to share more of what we have.

You can break this cycle simply. Choose just one item, something you've not used or worn for more than 12 months, and give it away. Give it to a relative or friend you know who could make use of it, or donate it to a charity shop that could sell it and put the proceeds to a good cause. You'll like the way you feel as a result. Do it again, and again.

Not only will you enjoy the feeling you get when you have less to guard and when you know someone is benefiting from what you've given away, you'll also find that you'll start to worry less about having enough for yourself. I can't explain why, but for some reason those who are unafraid to share always find that they have enough.

The trap of believing you need lots of choice

This trap is the notion that the more choices you can have, the happier you'll be and the more satisfied you'll feel. In fact, the opposite is true.

Too much of any one thing can slow you down, because it will take time to decide which of these items you'll choose on any particular occasion. If for example you have lots of clothes, it will take you longer to decide what to wear in the morning than it would if your choice was more limited. This is particularly true if you duplicate items – say you have a number of black trousers. Not only do you have to decide which colour trousers you want to wear, you also have to decide which one of that chosen colour you'll wear that day!

Not only is it more time consuming to weed through possibilities when you have too much choice. All those possibilities also make it harder to arrive at a final decision. This is best illustrated in a study in America that's come to be known as 'the jam experiment'.

In this experiment, researchers set up a stall in a grocery store in California and offered customers free samples of a gourmet jam. They laid out the stall in two different ways. In the first situation, they presented shoppers with six types of jam from which to choose. In the second, they offered them 24 types. Although there appeared to be little difference in the taste-testing behaviours of the shoppers, 30 per cent of those who visited the stall that offered six choices actually purchased some jam, whereas only *three* percent purchased jam after visiting the table that offered 24 choices.

And there's more. The experimenters decided to conduct a second experiment, this time to look at how satisfied customers feel once they've made a decision and purchased an item. In this experiment, subjects were given a choice of either six or 30 types of gourmet chocolate to taste. They were asked first whether they preferred to be given a larger or a more limited number of choices and then, once they'd made their decision, to rate how satisfied they felt with the choice they'd made. As you might expect, the overwhelming majority claimed that they'd rather have the larger number of choices. However, once they'd actually made their decision, the participants who were offered the greater number of choices reported *less satisfaction* with the choice they'd made than did those who chose from a more limited selection of chocolates!

The author Bill Bryson would no doubt agree. After living for some time in England, in 1996 he and his family moved back to America, a country that's proud to offer consumers as many choices as possible.

At first, Bryson was delighted by the 'wealth of choice everywhere' (*Notes from a Big Country*, p. 286), as he put it. Soon, however, he began to realise that there are serious drawbacks when there's too much of something. Here he is, waiting in a queue to purchase a cup of coffee early one morning at the airport in Portland, Oregon:

'When at last my turn came, I stepped up and said, "I'd like a large cup of coffee."'
'What kind?'
'Hot and in a cup and very large.'
'Yeah, but what kind – mocha, macchiato, what?'
'I want whichever one is a normal cup of coffee.'
'You want Americano?'
'If that means a normal cup of coffee, then yes.'
'Well, they're all coffees.'
'I want a normal cup of coffee like millions of people drink every day.'
'So you want an Americano?'

'Evidently.'
'Do you want low-cal whipped cream or regular with that?'
'I don't want whipped cream.'
'But it comes with whipped cream.'
'Look,' I said in a low voice, 'It is 6.10 a.m. I have been standing for 25 minutes behind fifteen seriously indecisive people and my flight is being called. If I don't get some coffee right now, I am going to murder someone, and I think you should know that you are extremely high on my list.' (I am not, as you will gather, a morning person.)
'So does that mean you want low-cal whipped cream or regular?'
And so it went.
This abundance of choice not only makes every transaction take ten times as long as it ought to, but in a strange way actually breeds dissatisfaction. The more there is, the more people crave, and the more they crave, the more they, well, crave more. You have a sense in America of being among millions of people needing more and more of everything, constantly, infinitely, unquenchably.'

(*Notes from a Big Country*, pp. 288–289)

The moral here is clear. Although you probably imagine that it's a 'good thing' to have more choices rather than fewer, in fact when you're faced with a great deal of choice you'll have more difficulty making up your mind. Furthermore, once you've made a choice, you'll feel less satisfied than you would if you'd had a more limited number of items from which to choose. When it comes to material goods, therefore, there's simply no justification for giving yourself more choices. Keep it simple!

How to reduce the clutter and increase your satisfaction

Once you decide that you're going to get rid of the things you don't really need, you'll feel a sense of relief. No one actually wants to be worrying about lots of items they seldom, if ever, use. It can, however, feel like an overwhelming task to declutter. You need to be systematic and to start small. Here's how:

Your clothing

This is a great place to start. Because you decide what to wear every day, you'll notice the difference almost straight away when you declutter your wardrobe.

Open your clothes closet and take a good look at the contents. Which items have you not worn for more than two years? Fashion experts will tell you that you're very unlikely ever to wear those items. Take them out of the wardrobe.

Now see if you can think of someone who might benefit from those items. Your sibling? A friend? Or perhaps you could offer the items to a charity shop, who can sell them and put the proceeds to a good cause. It's hard to part with things you've had for a long time, but the pleasure you'll get from choosing someone who might enjoy your gift will greatly outweigh any discomfort you may feel. Once again, Kahlil Gibran puts it wonderfully:

'*And to the open-handed the search for one who shall receive is joy greater than giving.*
And is there aught you would withhold?
All you have shall some day be given;
Therefore give now, that the season of giving may be yours and not your inheritors.'

If you'd like to make your life even calmer and your decisions in the morning even easier, divide your remaining clothing into two groups, the winter garments and those you only wear in the summer. Put those items that match the current season at the front of your wardrobe. Now check through the remaining items to make sure each is clean and in good repair, and put them either at the back of your wardrobe – or better yet, somewhere else entirely. That way, when the next season comes round, you'll get out what will feel like an entirely new wardrobe. Everything will be in good repair and ready to wear, and it won't have cost you a penny.

Finally, if you wish to be super-efficient, make a list of the items you own, noting the colours. Keep this list available whenever you're shopping, so you're not tempted to purchase an item that is in fact simply a duplication of something you already own. Vow, too, to choose colours that match the ones you already have. When the colours all blend, you can choose more freely which items you'd like to wear each day.

Your living space
The best approach is to go through your home systematically, and at such a pace that you can enjoy the

process and never feel overwhelmed. For example, choose one room each week.

Start by using your ability to be mindful and simply observe that room and its contents. Imagine you've never entered that room before, and note carefully everything that's in it. You may be surprised how much you really have. You may even discover some things you'd forgotten about and can now enjoy. If there are a great number of items in that room, you may wish to write them down.

On another occasion, go back to the room or get out your list and decide which items you need and which you enjoy frequently. The rest can go. Decide what you'd like to do with the superfluous items in the same way you did with the clothing you gave away. Finally, if you wish to be super-efficient, check through your remaining items to make sure they're serviceable and in good condition.

Your workplace

Most of us have a place where we work at home, and many of us also work elsewhere as well. Be sure to simplify these spaces as well. This may be a big job, so it's wise to allow perhaps a couple of weeks to go through each of your work spaces. Do just as you did for the other rooms. First, imagine that you're seeing the room, your files, your emails – everything – for the first time. Which items do you *really* need? Which could you do without? Take your time.

One patient I worked with had a business he ran jointly with another person. The two of them decided to declutter. They needed several months to sort their workspace!

However, when they were finished, they claimed that they'd never felt more organised. They also told me that they were getting along with one another better. Because they'd undertaken the difficult job of getting up to date together, they felt much more like equals, and a great deal of the resentment they'd felt towards one another disappeared.

Once you've finished your initial declutter, you'll want to keep things organised and as simple as possible. In the next section when you learn to plan ahead in the most helpful way, be sure to include a monthly 'declutter and reorganise' session in your schedule.

How to Declutter Physically

1. Acquaint yourself with the traps that encourage us all to keep more than we need.

2. In particular, think carefully about the distinction between 'wanting' and 'needing'. Consider which of your possessions make your life calmer and more balanced, and which create clutter and anxiety, demanding that you spend unnecessary time on them.

3. Declutter systematically. It's most rewarding to begin by decluttering your wardrobe.

4. From now on, include in your schedule regular occasions to review your possessions. Once every three months is a good interval to allow.

DECLUTTER PROCEDURALLY

In this section you'll learn how to streamline your schedule. Your aim is to get rid of unnecessary tasks, in particular those that only generate anxiety. As a result, you'll feel calmer and more relaxed and you'll be able to concentrate more fully on what you do decide to do and enjoy your life more.

However, before you start making any changes, it's important to become aware of more traps – this time, those that keep many of us locked into a punishing and ineffective schedule:

Three procedural traps

1. *The multitasking trap*

   Sadly, most people have bought into the idea that multitasking is the most efficient way to work. However, you now know (from Step One) that there's no such thing as 'multitasking' and that when we think we're doing several things at once, what's actually happening is that we're switching back and forth from one task to another. It actually means you'll take longer to complete those tasks than it would take if you focused your attention on and completed each of them in turn.

   Finally and most important, always remember that multitasking never pays off. Whenever you try it, you'll only end up working more slowly and feeling more agitated and stressed than if you do one thing at a time. No doubt it will be difficult at times to resist the pressure from other people to continue to multitask, particularly when you first start. You'll no doubt be told that you're going to become inefficient and 'fall behind'. You know, however, that's not true, and if ever you doubt it, go back to Step One and take the multitasking test again. Use your mindfulness training to anchor yourself, and persevere.

2. *The immediate response trap*
At first glance, it seems a sensible idea to respond straight away to emails, phone messages and texts. That way, you might think that you'll keep up to date and not build up a backlog of obligations.

Surprisingly, the opposite is true. This is the one time that actually waiting for a while before you respond to remote messaging is a more powerful way of keeping your workload under control than is 'keeping up to date'. Here's why:

The majority of messages these days are intended merely to establish or keep open a line of communication, rather than to ask any questions that demand an immediate response. If you answer that sort of email the sender will feel obligated to send a reply back to you – not to ask for information but simply to keep open the link between you.

What starts to happen under these circumstances is that the 'ping pong' of communication speeds up, while at the same time the content of the messages sent becomes increasingly pointless and uninformative. Worst of all, no one knows when to stop! Look back at a string of email or text of exchanges and you'll see what I mean.

Therefore, whenever you receive an email or a text message, read it mindfully. Just try to understand it. Don't try to compose an immediate response. Put it to one side and read it again later, and only then consider whether it warrants a response. If you think it does, decide how long you can wait before sending that response.

If you handle your remote communications in this manner, you'll find that you'll keep up far better with messaging than you will if you fire back instant responses.

3. *The 24/7 availability trap*

You may hold the belief that other people want to know that you're available whenever they need you. As a result, you probably keep your phones and other communication devices switched on and near you at all times. Except when you're told to turn them off, you probably also make sure the device will alert you immediately whenever someone tries to contact you. This is taken to such extremes that many individuals even take their phones to bed with them and keep them on all night.

This behaviour is based on a fallacy, and furthermore it's totally counter-productive. The fallacy is that you always need to be available to other people. This is unrealistic. No one other than a new-born baby really needs another individual to be constantly available to him or her. What we all do want to know, however, is *when* those who are important to us will be available. We also hope that during the times of availability, they'll give us their full attention.

I'm sure you can see another problem here. If you're always on call you'll let *everyone* who matters to you down because you'll never be able to give *any of them* your full attention. You'll also feel distracted, exhausted and directionless.

Instead of remaining constantly alert and flooding your system with anxiety-inducing stress hormones, stop and think. How often is 'often enough' to answer to those who need you? Again, unless you're looking after babies or young children, 'constantly' is not the right answer!

A much better and more satisfying approach is to establish two principles. First, earmark a regular time when you plan to give your loved ones your full attention. During that time, make sure all your communication devices are switched off. If you're raising children and/or live with a partner, try to ensure that this happens once every day, for example for half an hour after everyone is back from work and school. Your loved ones will revel in your undivided attention, and you'll feel better about yourself as a partner and/or parent. This is a quintessential example of mindfulness, of paying attention fully and in the present moment to those you care about most.

Second, with regard to everyone else, establish several reasonably frequent times each day when you'll answer messages and respond to requests. Make sure everyone knows what these are. The best way to do this is to create an appropriate message on each communication device, to let everyone know when you'll be in contact. In between those times put incoming messages on 'silent' so you can focus your attention on the things you want and need to do.

Here's a nice example of how a stressed out businessman called James dealt with his anxiety and re-established his ability to concentrate. The example is taken from Dave Crenshaw's book *The Myth of Multitasking*. After consulting the author about his inability to control his workload, James re-recorded this phone message for use at work:

'Hello, this is James. You've reached my voice mail, which means I'm probably meeting with a customer right now. I do check my messages frequently, usually at 10 a.m., 2 p.m. and 4 p.m. If you leave a message, I will be sure to get back to you before the day is over. Thank you.'

(*The Myth of Multitasking*, p. 60)

Streamlining your schedule

The first step to gaining space in your schedule is to get rid of backlogs. As you've now learned, that doesn't mean answering every message immediately! It does, however, mean you'll need to set aside time to look through your messages and piles of papers. Just as when you decluttered physically, make sure you don't overload yourself and try to sort out everything at once. Take it at a comfortable pace.

When you sort, the best rule to use is the '4D Rule':

Do It,
Delegate It,
Defer It, or
Dump It.

In other words, if the item will take you less than ten minutes to accomplish, do it right then.

If it's possible that someone else can do it, delegate it appropriately.

If you're certain that only you can do whatever it is and that the need still exists, earmark a time when you'll attend to it, and then set it aside.

Dump the rest.

Now that you've cleared the clutter, establish a period of time each day when you can be fully attentive to your loved ones. Next, choose the times when you'll check your messages and respond to them. Record a message to let everyone know when you'll be in touch, and resolve firmly to stick to your plan.

How to Declutter Procedurally

1. Clear away accumulated messages and requests. Sort these using the 4D Rule: Do it right then (if it will take less than ten minutes); Delegate it (if you can); or Defer it (if it's a bigger job and you're certain that you're the only one who can do it). Dump everything else.

2. Establish a period of time each day when you'll give your full attention to those who matter most to you.

3. Whenever possible, decide in advance when you'll check your messages and answer requests. Try to stick to this plan, so that in between responding you can focus fully on the tasks at hand. On those occasions when you must be constantly available to others, don't try to 'fit in' other tasks, because you'll only become less efficient and feel more stressed if you do.

4. Avoid the traps that can cause you to be inefficient and ineffective. Remember:

    a) Multitasking is a myth and switchtasking is ineffective.
    b) If you're always waiting to respond, you'll never be able to concentrate fully on what you want to do.
    c) Other people don't need you to be constantly available. They only want to know that they can contact you, and when you'll reply.

It's time now to learn how to make plans that you can realistically expect to fulfil.

PLANNING REALISTICALLY

It would indeed be heavenly to spend every moment of your life fully absorbed in the present, with no awareness of yesterday or worries about tomorrow. That is, as I understand it, the definition of Enlightenment, and I believe that the only individual who ever managed to achieve it was Buddha.

For the rest of us, however, living in the modern world means we have to think about the future, and we have to spend some time making plans. Of course, you'll still want to set aside periods of time every day to be fully mindful. The 'mindful moments' will revive and refresh you. They'll also increase your ability to concentrate when you wish to do so and to withhold judgment until it's appropriate to offer any. They will, in other words, allow you to see ahead with greater clarity and to formulate more realistic and workable plans.

In this section, you'll learn to plan your schedule in ways that will guarantee a sense of accomplishment, pride and satisfaction, but that at the same time won't make you feel constricted or tied down. You'll find that, despite the freedom you will be offered when you use my approach, you'll accomplish at least as much as you would do if you'd made plans according to more traditional methods of timetabling.

My approach is unusual, so it's best if you discard your notion of a traditional schedule right now.

Instead, this is how to plan ahead realistically. This procedure is adapted from a system I developed to help students when they are preparing for exams at school and University. It will 'cost' you about 15 minutes a week (30 minutes the first time you do it). The payback for this regular investment is enormous. You'll find that it will decrease your stress levels significantly because you no longer need to worry about whether you'll remember to do the things you need to do, or whether you'll have enough time to fit everything in. It's also energising because, as well as getting through the necessities without undue pressure, you'll also start doing some of the things you've always hoped to do.

Start by setting aside a 15 minute 'planning time' each week. Make sure you'll be uninterrupted. You might choose a time when you'd stop for a cup of coffee or tea anyway, right after work on a particular day, or just after the children are in bed. Make this a regular time – that way it will become a good habit more quickly. Most of my clients set aside time on a Sunday afternoon or evening, because that's when most of them are naturally thinking about the week ahead.

There are four steps you need to follow. The first time you work through them, the first step will probably take you about half an hour. However, because the template you'll create is unlikely to vary much from week to week, from then on you'll only need to allow about five minutes for this step. You may wish to create two templates, one for weekdays and one for weekends. If you have school-aged children you may also decide to create one template to use during term and one during the school holidays.

Here, then, are some steps that will help you plan realistically, reduce your stress levels, and enjoy life more fully:

The basics: create your templates

Open your diary. Note your normal waking time and bedtime each day. These two times 'frame' your day, and they give you the number of hours you have available. For example, if you go to bed at 11 p.m. and get up at 7 a.m. you have 16 hours to work with each weekday. At weekends your 'frame' may look rather different – if so, create the weekend template as well. If you have school-aged children and your schedule during the school holidays is quite different than it is during term times, then create a 'school holidays' template as well.

Now fill in the fixed items – in other words, the hours you're at work and the times you take the children to and from school, the times you attend classes yourself and/ or perhaps look after an elderly relative, and any other regular, fixed items you attend to each week. Make sure you include the travel times to and from your destinations in the templates.

On a separate piece of paper make a list of all other weekly chores and activities that are regular and necessary fixtures, for example the food shopping, cooking, house cleaning and laundry. Be sure to fill in meal times, as well as the time you need to get ready in the morning and to wind down at night. Estimate the amount of time you usually spend on each item.

Then – before you add these to your timetable – consider whether you could do any of the items listed more economically. For example, if you're in the habit of doing your food shopping three times a week, think about whether you could combine two of those trips into one and ask your partner to do the third. Consider whether you might do the cleaning only once a week, or cook a number of meals at the weekend and put some in the freezer, and so on. Now write these items into your templates.

You've now created your basic framework, the 'bones' of your schedule that takes into account all the things you do each week. As a result, in the coming weeks, your first step will be quick and easy. Simply choose the appropriate template, take a minute to make sure that there are no changes coming up, add in anything particular for that week (for example, a dental appointment), and then proceed to the next step.

Establish your own priorities

Put your template aside for now. Close your eyes and relax, or just let your mind wander away from schedules and timetables for a moment or two. Think about your strengths and passions, the things you discovered about yourself in Step Three.

Now make a new list. Write down all the things you'd *like* to work on during the coming week. We're no longer talking about the things you know you *have* to do – you can forget about them because you've taken them into account already. Now it's time to let yourself think about what you'd *like* to spend some time doing, those activities that aren't necessary but that you know would help you feel more fulfilled and complete.

For example, perhaps there's a new book out that you'd love to read. Maybe you want to take a Pilates class, meet up with a friend, learn a new language, plan a holiday for next summer or just spend an hour day-dreaming.

Don't worry about whether these items are big projects or small tasks. Try, too, to avoid thinking about how long it might take to complete any one of these activities. Simply list the items you'd like to focus on, in whatever order that they come into your mind.

Now arrange your wishes in order. Start with the one that appeals to you most, then the second most interesting and so on, until they're all accounted for. Each week, you'll concentrate on the first three on your list.

Don't be surprised, by the way, when you start to notice your list changing from week to week. It may be, for example, that you once thought you'd love to learn to play the piano. However, after a couple of lessons you realise that it's not as interesting as you'd thought it would be. That's fine. Take 'learning to play the piano' off your list.

When something new comes to mind, add it to your list.

Remember, this isn't a list of obligations that you 'should' do or that you have to carry out to completion come what may. This is *your* time, time for you to explore possibilities and learn more about yourself.

Start living your dreams

It's time now to pick up your template again. Have a look at each day to find the gaps in your schedule. Where is there an opportunity to spend some time on one of your top three priorities? If the gaps of time are small, you may have to become rather creative about what you choose to do! Don't, however, let that discourage you.

Say for example that you can see half an hour free on Wednesday afternoon. You indicated that your top priority this week is to take a course on bread making. Obviously, you can't fit an entire course into half an hour! Therefore, you might decide to take a look at item two or three on your wish list instead.

On the other hand, you could still do something about the bread-making idea if you prefer. For example, you could put on that DVD that came with your new book on bread baking and watch it for half an hour. Or you might look for relevant video clips on the internet. Or you could ring a friend who you know is brilliant at baking and ask her where she buys her flour.

You may, if you're extremely busy on a particular week, have to accept that you have no gaps at all during that week. Even so, most of us will have some time free during the weekend. If that's the case this week, find some opportunities to fit in some priority time during the weekend.

However, before you accept that every weekday is completely booked, have another look at your template. Is *everything* you've included really necessary? Are you really being as efficient as you might be? Could you, for example, amalgamate some tasks or delegate some of them to others? Are you trying to multitask, or in other ways are you unwittingly slowing yourself down, say by leaving the TV on while you're trying to do other things? Are there any 'shoulds' in your schedule that you'd be better off eliminating?

It's worth taking that second look, because you may well find that, with some careful thought and creative planning, you can free up time for yourself, even if it's only half an hour or an hour during the entire week. You'll find that this is self-reinforcing because you're putting your own wishes on a par with the demands from everyone else. It's also a fact that when you spend some time *on a frequent basis,* doing the things you love, you'll find that you have more energy to do everything else, and the less stressful you'll consider your life to be more enjoyable.

Finally, take a moment, right now, to write your priorities into your template for the current week. This is extremely important because it will prevent them being stolen away by 'shoulds'. It will also make it easier for you to say 'no' if you need to fend off a request to do something else, something you don't really want to do, but you feel you might be compelled to do if you noticed a space for it in your diary. Write in what you've chosen to do – 'yoga practice', or 'gardening', or 'study time' – or if you prefer, simply write 'MT' for 'me time'.

Remember, it doesn't matter how *much* time you have available to spend on your priorities each week. I've had clients who sometimes find only half an hour free during the entire seven days. What does matter is that you're starting to do something that's just for you – and you're doing it *now*. Keep Goethe's words in mind:

'Whatever you do, or dream you can, begin it!
Boldness has genius, magic and power in it.
Begin it now!'

Allocating time for your own priorities will generate a powerful and positive feeling. You'll feel calmer, and you'll start to feel more in control of your life.

How to Plan Realistically

1. Establish a 15-minute uninterrupted period of time each week to think about your schedule for the next seven days. Be sure to consider your own priorities as well as your obligations. Sunday afternoon or evening is best. Make this time sacrosanct.

2. Create templates for weekdays and for weekend days, term weeks and holiday weeks. These templates take account of everything you need to do on a typical day. Make copies so they're ready to use when you make your plans each week.

3. During your weekly planning period, create a wish list of the things *you* want to do. Prioritise your list.

4. Fill in as many gaps in your template as you can with any of the top three items from your wish list each week. Do NOT specify or demand particular accomplishments! These are times for exploration and fulfilment, opportunities for trying out and for exploration. They are not there so you can cross off goals or impress others.

LEARNING HOW TO SAY 'NO' EFFECTIVELY

It's very common to become inspired to make changes, to feel determined to change, but then to find that you give up. As soon as you clear the time and space to make changes, someone makes a request on your time and you find yourself saying 'yes' without taking time first to consider whether the request is important enough to take priority over your own resolve.

How can you stop that instant reaction, so you have time to consider the practicalities of whatever it is that you've been asked to do?

This last section is designed to help you break the bad 'yes' habit, so you can stick with your good intentions and start to spend time in ways that allow you to enjoy yourself more, and to feel in more control of your life. Here are three guidelines to help you:

1. *Look at things from the other person's point of view*
The inability to say 'no' is a particular weakness for those of you who feel that it's really important to please other people. You assume that you'll only please others if you always try to oblige them. The truth, however, is that this approach is less effective than you might imagine.

The best way to ensure that other people are pleased and delighted when you're around is to be relaxed and confident in their company. In other words, if you know what's important to you and you value your needs as least as much as the needs of others, you'll become a happier, calmer and more pleasant person. Other people will want to be with you.

Think about the people you know. Who would you prefer to spend time with? Is it someone who's constantly on the alert, ready and anxious to please you? Or would you rather be with someone who appears to know his or her own mind, who does what pleases them and really enjoys life?

By looking at things from outside yourself I hope you'll see that when you value yourself and stick with your priorities, you'll be deemed far more attractive and fun to be with than if you're always trying to make everybody else happy, never mind the cost to you.

2. *Give yourself time to consider the request*
You've already made a good start, by allocating a time every week to sort out and write out your schedule. Make sure, therefore, that you *always* include that 15-minute slot in your weekly template to decide how you'll arrange your week and that you *write in* your 'me time' when you're filling in everything else. That way, if you're put on the spot with a request, answer that you'll have to check your availability. Then later, you can say honestly that that particular time slot is filled already. That's the way to avoid making a decision under pressure.

Later, if you decide that you'd *rather* do what was asked of you (not that you *should* do it, by the way, only that you'd prefer to do it rather than what you had written down), then you can always contact the person who made the request and say that you've rearranged your schedule so that you can now join him or her.

3. *Keep your explanation simple*
If you're unsure of yourself, particularly if you're also anxious to please, you'll no doubt feel the need to justify a refusal. This is a trap. As soon as you start elaborating,

you'll appear defensive, and the person you're talking with is likely to encourage you to change your plans.

Therefore, the best answer is always the simple one, the one that doesn't invite argument. You only need to say, 'I'm so sorry, but no, I can't manage that.' If you then feel an overwhelming desire to justify yourself, take a slow breath in through your nose and hold it, then exhale just as slowly. Repeat. Then change the subject.

At first, this direct approach may seem difficult. However, as you practise, you'll start to feel proud that you can give your own needs and priorities the importance they deserve.

How to Say 'No' and Mean It

1. Each week, during your scheduling period, write into your diary the things you really want to do, at the times that are available for you to do them.

2. When you meet with an unexpected request, explain that you'll have to consult your diary. If the time slot needed to meet the request is already filled, turn down the request (barring true emergencies of course).

3. Say no simply: 'No, I'm sorry but I can't do that.' There's no need to justify your refusal.

Step Five:
Reach Out

'No man is an island, entire of itself.
Each is a piece of the continent, a part of the main'
John Donne

f Steps One to Four have now become part of your life, you'll no doubt be feeling calmer, happier and more positive, perhaps more so than you've felt for years.

You won't, however, feel fully satisfied. Even though you're now healthier and you know yourself better, even though you can now concentrate well and enjoy the moment without judging it, and even though you've streamlined your life and feel more in control, still you will feel as if 'something' is missing.

That's because it is. It's time now to infuse your new, calmer and more contented way of living with a sense of wholeness and deeper meaning.

To feel fully satisfied and balanced human beings need to reach out, to feel part of a larger group and to know that they're not alone. This allows us to feel safe, and when we're safe we can relax and feel calm.

This step will show you how to incorporate this vital

need into your everyday life. Once you've done so, you really will have discovered the Key to Calm. At that point, not only will you be calmer and happier, you'll also feel balanced and complete.

Here, then, is the last ingredient you need to regain your sense of calm, the step that will give meaning and direction to everything you've learned so far, as well as to all you have yet to encounter.

Socialising is essential for the formation of a healthy identity

Over the course of your life, you'll invent and re-invent yourself many times. Your first task as an infant was to separate your identity from that of your mother. As a toddler and pre-schooler, you were most interested in identifying yourself as a boy or a girl, and you became aware of your place in your family.

When you started school, you learned the ways in which you differed from and were similar to your classmates. Your race, accent, and perhaps your religious affiliation became important. As a teenager, you sought a peer group identity, dressing and talking like other members of your chosen 'group'.

Only towards the end of adolescence did you really begin to carve out your *individual* identity, answering these questions:

'Who am I in ways that are *unlike* everyone else I know?'
'What makes me unique?'

'What are my particular gifts and talents, and how can I apply them?'

'What career is best for me?'

'Who (if anyone) do I wish to choose to be my long-term partner?'

All these questions can only be answered in relationship to other individuals. You can only really know yourself by comparing yourself to others, by choosing to identify with certain other people, and at the same by establishing yourself as unique among them.

On the one hand, we seek to belong, to know that we're part of a group – or more often, several groups – whose members value and depend upon one another. This allows us to feel safe. At the same time, however, we endeavour to establish individuality, to stand out from the others in our groups. After all, when something is unique, it's more easily noticeable and seems more valuable.

The formation of identity, a crucial aspect of good psychological health, therefore depends on spending time with other people and learning about them.

The importance of family

In 1977, ABC TV in America ran a mini-series called *Roots*. Based on a novel written by Alex Haley, it told the story of young man called Kunta Kinte who was captured by slave traders in 1750. The programme followed him as he was transported to America and sold into slavery, then focused on his descendants, ending the story in 1870. A sequel, *Roots: The Next Generations* followed in 1979.

The series was a sensation, watched by over a million people, and it received nine Emmy awards.

Roots is most notable because it dramatised slavery and in particular because it showed, probably for the first time publically, the brutality of the practice of keeping slaves. However, the other story line – the idea of tracing your ancestry far back in time to discover where you've come from and who your ancestors were – captured the imagination of millions and it started many on a deeper search for their identity. The writer Kwame Kwei-Armah describes such a quest:

> *'Thirty years ago I was an 11-year-old growing up in West London. One evening I sat down with my family to watch a new television programme called 'Roots'.*
>
> *It was a moment that changed my life. By the end of the series I had told my mother that I would one day trace my heritage back to Africa and reclaim an ancestral name. Before I watched the programme I was called Ian Roberts but now my name is Kwame Kwei-Armah.'*
>
> (*BBC News Magazine*, 23 March 2007)

Today, tracing your family history is big business. You're probably familiar with the TV series, *Who Do You Think You Are?*, where in each episode a celebrity learns about thev people in their past. Online, if you google 'tracing family history', you'll come up with 5,390,000 hits in less than a second. Amazon currently advertises 621 hardcover and 1,736 paperback books on the subject, and the BBC has a dedicated Family History website, devoted entirely to helping you trace your family history.

Of course, tracing your genealogy isn't the only way to understand yourself better. As I've said in Step Three, one of the most enjoyable ways to learn more about yourself is to ask those who've known you for a long time what you were like as a child. This person is most likely to be a grandparent or great-grandparent. However, other relatives, long-time family friends and others who've in any way played an important role in your life can also help.

Furthermore, you'll not be the only one who will benefit from such questions. Asking others to share their knowledge makes them feel useful and valued. My own father, for example, has (at 87 years of age) taken on a new lease of life as a 'storyteller' in the primary school in his local neighbourhood. The kids love him and the stories he has to tell, and he loves telling tales of how things used to be. This has helped him make more sense of his own existence.

We all yearn to understand better who we are, and one of the best ways to do that is by understanding where we came from. This helps us relate with more confidence to other people and, therefore, start to build the friendship circle we all need.

Thus self-understanding has a dual purpose. It helps you understand yourself better and to establish your unique identity, and it allows you to feel safe by knowing that you're a part of a wider community.

Why it feels so good to know that you belong

No doubt you've heard a defiant three-year-old exclaim as she pushes her mother aside, 'I do it MYSELF!' Or you've been told by the angry teenager whom you've offered to help that you should just 'go away and leave me ALONE!'

These are healthy expressions, expressions of our need to learn how to work through problems and challenges unassisted. After all, the major goal throughout childhood and adolescence is to learn how to figure things out for oneself so you can become independent.

However, only moments later that same defiant toddler will hold out her arms to be picked up and cuddled, and sometime later that sulky teenager will thank you for your concern – even if grudgingly. That's because, although we need to know we can solve problems alone, we are also aware that we very much need each other.

Human beings depend on others of their own kind in order to survive, and they do so for relatively longer than does any other creature on earth. Whereas many insects are born fully formed, birds fly from the nest within a few months of hatching, and even most large mammals are standing and walking within a day of birth, human babies are totally dependent on their carers for many months. In fact, they're still fairly dependent on them even after nine or ten years.

This interdependency wasn't an evolutionary 'mistake'. In fact, the payoff for our initial immaturity is that we humans are able to develop and fit in perfectly to almost any environment. The human brain can adapt and change throughout our lives, of course, but never as readily and as effortlessly as it does when we're very young.

This initial plasticity allows human beings to thrive in incredibly varying conditions, to learn any number of languages, and to learn to live with a wider variety of customs and practices than can any other animal.

In short, we're able to acquire the problem-solving skills we need and to do so in almost any environmentin which we find ourselves. We do it, however, not through independence, but with help at times – that is, through *inter*dependence.

That's why it feels so good to know that there are others around who care about us and whom we care about, even when we're completely focused on figuring something out on our own. If ever we have the *need* to do so, we want to know that there's someone around we can turn to because when we were young – we needed someone *all* the time. The human brain hasn't forgotten this truth, and it 'rewards' us when we come together by releasing more of the chemicals that encourage us to bond with others (such as oxytocin), as well as by suppressing those that make us feel anxious and stressed (cortisol).

Additional benefits of knowing that you belong

There are numerous payoffs when you make the effort to form and maintain your relationships, far more even than those I've just described.

If you socialise regularly with people you value and like, you'll be more robust psychologically. In particular, you'll be less likely to become depressed or to suffer from stress or anxiety. Your immune system will remain stronger than it would otherwise have done and, as a consequence, you're more likely to remain healthy and to fight off chronic disease.

You'll experience greater pleasure, because the best pleasures are those that are exchanged rather than merely taken.

And certainly not least, you'll feel safe and secure – a state of mind that will afford you the best chance to relax, to be creative and to have fun.

Let's look at the some of the work that's been done to back up these claims.

Social support as a buffer against depression

In the mid-1908s, G.W. Brown and his colleagues carried out a study in London that looked carefully at the relationship between social support, levels of self-confidence and the risk of becoming depressed. The researchers interviewed a number of women in London, all of whom had at least one child under 18 living at home with them. The sample covered a broad age range and included both single mums and those living with a partner.

Each woman met twice with an interviewer, initially and then again a year later. The aim of the first interview was to obtain a psychiatric history from each of the women, to measure how self-confident she seemed and to determine the strength of her personal relationships. At the second meeting, interviewers asked each woman whether she'd suffered any psychological problems, in particular if she'd become depressed during the last 12 months. They also asked her to tell them about any life stressors, such as problems with their health or finances or within their relationships, and what support they felt they'd received from friends and family.

What Brown and his colleagues found – as you might expect – was that those women who experienced a stressful life event were more likely to become depressed than were the other women. Furthermore, those who had a poor self-image were particularly vulnerable to becoming depressed, as you might also have guessed.

However – and this is the key finding for our purposes – of the women who did suffer a stressful life event, those who had a partner, close friend or relative who supported them through the crisis had a significantly *lower* chance of becoming depressed than those who were not supported. Thus this study shows that social support can make people less vulnerable to depression.

There's plenty more evidence that socialising can help protect us from becoming depressed. Another study was carried out in Dublin by postdoctoral psychologists Joanna McHugh and Brian Lawlor. They asked 583 older adults about various aspects of their current lifestyle including such things as the amount of exercise they took, the hobbies they enjoyed and what sorts of social support they had.

The researchers also asked these individuals about their mood state, that is, whether they suffered from depression, anxiety or stress.

What McHugh and Lawlor found was that both exercise and good social support were associated with lower scores on all three of the mood measures.

Here, then, is yet more evidence that good social support can lower the risk of becoming depressed – and this time the population studied included both men and women.

Social support and longevity

It seems that spending time enjoyably with other people may well offer more than just good psychological support. A study based at Harvard University found that an active and happy social life is also associated with a longer life.

These researchers interviewed more than 2,700 older men and women in Connecticut. They interviewed these individuals annually for thirteen years and kept records of their participation in 14 activities including exercise (for example, walking and swimming), self-care (shopping, running errands and the like) and socialising (for example, playing cards, getting together with friends, and doing voluntary work). Their aim was to find which of these activities was most strongly correlated with living a long life.

What they found was that those individuals who spent time plenty of time socialising survived well –

just as well, in fact, as those who exercised regularly. They concluded that social engagement was as strong as exercise in determining how long a person lived. Indeed, the correlation between a longer life and frequent, high quality social activity was even higher than the correlation between longevity and records of subjects' blood pressure levels, cholesterol, and other measures of health.

There's other, even stronger evidence that socialising enjoyably with other people correlates well with good health and long life. One researcher even went so far as to say that good social networks actually, directly, help us live longer. If you wish to learn more about the relationship between socialising, health and longevity, you'll find a number of studies listed in the References section.

I've seen plenty of evidence to back up this research in my clinics. One of my patients, Richard, changed his entire outlook on what it means to 'age' when, at 70 years of age, he encountered an old school friend. This friend was two years older than Richard but, as Richard explained, 'he looked 20 years younger'. The secret, he told Richard, was that he had been meeting up twice a year with a group of friends to take holidays all over Europe. Planning these trips kept the group in touch between trips, and the desire to remain fit enough for sightseeing kept them all exercising in between. Richard joined the group immediately and when I last heard from him he was, at 78 years of age, healthy, cheerful and active.

However, I've never seen as dramatic a change as with Anna. Anna came to see me because she felt constantly exhausted. Every day, she said, it was a struggle just to get out of bed. She felt despondent and had no clear idea of the future.

Three years earlier, when she was only in her early thirties, Anna had lost her partner to cancer. She had nursed him through two agonising years while at the same time looking after their two young sons. Anna told me that gradually she had withdrawn from all social contact, focusing entirely on her partner and her children. In some ways, she'd had little choice, because she certainly had no immediate family to call upon. She had been born in central Europe, and her family had moved on numerous occasions, never staying long enough in one place to put down roots. Her birth family was now scattered, and none was living in the UK. In fact, Anna had herself only come to this country six years previously.

When Andrew died Anna resolved to 'be both mother and father' to her boys. No doubt she did an admirable job, but her social isolation was making her feel hopeless and depressed about her own future. Furthermore, she refused to take time for herself, to face up squarely to her loss and go through the necessary grieving process because, as Anna put it, 'I couldn't bear that pain all alone.'

We began by looking for ways, however small, that Anna could start to rebuild her social life. With great courage she decided to join a small parents' group based at her school. She also began inviting her neighbour, an elderly widow, over for coffee.

As Anna's sense of social connectedness grew she began to be able to talk about Andrew, about his death and the loss she had suffered. No longer having to work so hard to block her grief, Anna began to feel less tired. She looked healthier, and she told me with delight that her appetite had returned and she was enjoying her food again. She volunteered as a teaching assistant at her children's school, and later she also joined a yoga class. Gradually, her depression lifted and her energy returned. Now when I see Anna in town she seems always to be smiling, and her children are usually accompanied by friends.

Does it matter *how* you choose to socialise?

Yes, it matters a great deal how you decide to spend your time when you socialise – both in terms of how you socialise and with whom. We now know that some forms of socialising will actually cause you to feel *more* stressed and anxious, rather than less so. Let's take a look at which circumstances are most likely to allow you to be healthier and happier, and which are more likely to leave you feeling more anxious and stressed.

Socialising with regard to your personality

In Step Three we looked at those characteristics that appear to be highly genetic – in other words, those that are a consistent aspect of your makeup. The one that's important when considering the best way for you to socialise is the introversion-extroversion dimension.

If you're an extrovert, then the most beneficial way for you to socialise is to spend time with groups of friends, probably doing something active and that takes you into the wider community or – perhaps even better – something that does both. Parties, adventures, community activities, group outings – these are for you.

If, on the other hand, you're an introvert, then quieter, more intimate social occasions involving one or at most a few friends are better for you. Preparing a meal with a good friend, volunteering to befriend someone who's infirm or lonely – these are your best choices.

Who you socialise with

A number of the studies that examine the effect of socialising on our health point out that some types of relationships are better for us than others. If you spend time with people who let you down when you need them, or who make you feel inferior or less good about yourself, then you may be no better off, both psychologically and physically, than if you were more isolated.

The conclusion, therefore, is obvious – whenever possible, spend time with the people you love and trust and/or with people you know you can help in some way.

That's easy to suggest. However, there will be occasions when you need to spend time with people who don't make you feel better. When that's inevitable there are ways you can mitigate any deleterious effects they may have on your wellbeing.

1. *Meet up on your own territory*

   One approach is to arrange to meet in your own home or office. We usually feel stronger and safer in our own surroundings than we do when we're in someone else's 'territory'. If that's not possible, arrange to meet in a public area, at a restaurant or in the middle of town, for example. People are more likely to remain civil and polite when they're in public spaces. So, for example, if you have to meet up with a relative who always criticises you, suggest that you meet him or her for lunch in your favourite café.

2. *Include a loyal friend in the group whenever possible*

   Try, too, if you are meeting as a group that someone you like and trust is among the group. For example, if you're attending a business meeting when you know you'll be scrutinised or questioned in a challenging way, make sure a loyal and reliable colleague will be there as well so you can feel that you have some support.

3. *Set aside time to 'detox' from a stressful occasion*

   Finally, if possible, arrange to meet with a supportive friend, or in some other way take time to 'detox' after you've done your duty. One couple I worked with made an excellent arrangement. Whenever they visited her relatives they knew that those relatives would constantly criticise this woman's partner, comparing him unfavourably to her brother.

   Therefore, what they always arranged to do was to make the visit as short as was polite. Also, even though the in-laws only lived 100 miles away, the couple always booked an overnight stay in a nice B&B on the way home. Over dinner they would talk through the visit, doing their best to make light of hurtful moments and supporting one another. By doing this they felt they could 'leave it behind' in the B&B before they arrived home. This not only eased any negative effect the relatives' jibes might have had, it also strengthened the bond between the two of them.

The method of communication you choose

The sense of wellbeing and security we feel when we spend time with people who matter to us actually has little to do with what we say to one another. The most reassuring cues are actually the non-verbal ones – the touch, the kindly tone of voice, the laughter, even a familiar scent.

Human beings crave contact that's direct and personal. This seems to be something we've overlooked recently and it comes as no surprise to me that, as a result, more people than ever before report that they're feeling lonely. Being 'in touch' doesn't mean much when it's only an instant text message.

To feel fully appreciated, safe and cared for, we need to be in the company of others regularly. We feel truly safe only when we can sense the actual presence of those who matter most to us. We need regularly to experience their scent, to feel their kindly touch, to hear their familiar laughter and to see them smile.

The more removed we feel we are from the person we're

communicating with, the less benefit that communication will offer us. If we rank in order methods of communication from the least satisfying to the most it will, therefore, look like this:

1. Totally remote
   Instant messaging
   Texts
   Emails
   Social network sites

2. Remote but with voice
   Telephone calls

3. Remote but with voice and image
   Skype

4. Face-to-face encounters

Laura Donnelly, health correspondent for the *Sunday Telegraph*, offers some strong evidence to support the suggestion that remote communication is less than reassuring. In her article entitled, 'How Twitter can turn to fluster', Donnelly writes that a study found that 'social networking websites such as Facebook and Twitter feed anxiety and make people feel inadequate'. (*Daily Telegraph*, 8 July 2012, p. 17).

The article reports a poll of those who use these social networking websites. More than half of the participants claimed that the sites had changed their behaviour, and 50 per cent reported that their lives had been altered for the worse.

In particular, respondents claimed that their confidence had fallen after comparing their own achievements with those of online 'friends'. Two thirds found it hard to relax or get to sleep after using the websites. 25 per cent said they faced problems in their relationships or at work after becoming confrontational online.

Finally, many had fears that they were becoming addicted to checking the sites: 55 per cent admitted that they felt 'worried or uncomfortable' when they could not access Facebook or email accounts.

On the whole, it appears that communicating online offers fewer advantages than disadvantages.

If that's not enough to discourage you, it's also been suggested that we tend to misunderstand the sentiments in email and text communications – and in particular, to underestimate the warmth intended. Therefore, when you receive a text or email message it will, more often than not, leave you feeling *less* sure that the person you're communicating with cares about you or has your best interests at heart.

What this means is that all day long you may be investing time and energy in an activity that only leaves you feeling anxious and insecure. Why do it? At least if you speak to someone on the phone you can pick up reassuring verbal cues, and that's true even if what's said is the same as it would have been in the text or the email. Better yet, you could arrange to meet up and enjoy a good coffee and a face-to-face conversation.

Ten suggestions to help you get started

By now I'm sure you accept how important it is to communicate with and meet up with people whose company you enjoy. I hope, therefore, that you'll make it a priority to allow time in your schedule for this pleasure. I hope, too, that you've begun to think of some truly beneficial ways to reach out to others. Such activities needn't take 'extra' time. Many can be easily incorporated into your daily activities.

To help you get started, here's a list of ten suggestions that can add a great deal of quality to your life, without at the same time carving out lots of extra time in your schedule. You can use these suggestions as they stand, or you can adapt them so they're more suitable to your own circumstances. Better yet, you can simply use them as a starting point from which you generate ideas of your own.

1. *Make sure one of your mindful sessions involves socialising*
   By now, you're no doubt well-practised and therefore good at relaxing and focusing on the moment. In fact you're probably spending a fair amount of time each day doing just that. Why not dedicate one of those 'sessions' to someone you love?

   For example, take advice from the section on decluttering procedurally in the last chapter. Turn off all communication devices as soon as you come home from work and spend the first half hour listening, fully and attentively, to what your partner and children have to say about their day. They'll appreciate feeling so valued and you'll no doubt learn a great deal!

Whenever you meet up with a friend, make it a regular habit to turn off your phone and other communication devices when you're speaking with one another. I'm sure you know how devalued you feel if, when talking with a friend, his or her phone rings and you completely lose their attention. Try not to put others in that uncomfortable position.

As Thich Nhat Hanh reminds us, the ultimate goal of mindfulness practice is, after all, to make it *the way you live,* rather than something you set aside particular times to practise:

'*Be mindful 24 hours a day, not just during the one hour you may allot for formal meditation.'*

(*The Miracle of Mindfulness*, p. 24)

2. *Arrange once a week to meet up with a friend, face-to-face*

As you now know, a face-to-face meeting with one person you really like will leave you feeling happier, calmer and more socially connected than if you spend twice as long texting and sending emails to all the other people you know. Meeting for lunch is often a good arrangement because it feels like such a treat to sit down and enjoy what's so often a hurried meal.

Another possibility would be to invite a friend over and make dinner together. If you and the friend you'd like to see both have young children you could meet up with the kids so they can play together while you talk. If you and your friend are both dog lovers you might take a dog walk together.

I often advise couples I'm working with to arrange to 'date' one another again. This is a great excuse for a nice evening out! Do this once a fortnight and take it in turns to surprise each other with what you plan to do that evening.

3. *Telephone or Skype someone you've not been in touch with for a while*
This is an especially nice thing to do with friends and family who live so far away that you're rarely able to meet up in person. It will also mean that you keep up with a wide range of people.

This is beneficial because if you're in touch with a number of different people – friends of different ages, those who come from different backgrounds or those with whom you've shared particular experiences – then there will almost always be someone you can contact if ever you're hoping for particular advice or guidance. No doubt you'll fulfil that role for them at the same time.

4. *Be aware of the needs of others and offer to help if you can*
This seems so natural and so obvious that it wouldn't need saying. Yet, so often, we miss opportunities to lend a hand

because we don't really *look*. We glance at others, without thinking, and then return to our own thoughts.

Once again, you can use your ability to be mindful to help you spot opportunities to reach out. One of my clients found a lovely way to help a neighbour. This particular woman is very elderly and now housebound. My client used to visit her from time to time, and at one point the woman mentioned how much she missed reading a daily newspaper.

Now, every morning when my client takes her dog for an early walk, she stops by the local shop and buys a newspaper for her neighbour. She then drops it by her house on the way home. The entire exercise takes only a moment or two more than she'd have normally spent walking her dog. However, her gesture has made all the difference to her neighbour's quality of life.

5. *Thank someone sincerely if you notice they've gone to some effort to help you*

    This will cost you effectively no time at all, but it may change the other person's day completely. If, for example, someone helps you pick up something you dropped or steps aside so you can pass, thank him or her warmly instead of hurrying on or merely acknowledging the gesture with a brief nod. Other people enjoy feeling appreciated just as much as you do. Why not, therefore, give that pleasure to others?

6. *Compliment someone genuinely*

    This only works if you mean what you say. If, for

example, you tell your daughter that her hair looks great when you actually think it looks untidy, she'll probably notice the insincerity and as a result feel hurt and patronised – worse than if you'd said nothing.

You can always, always find *something* nice to say about someone else. You simply need to observe others more carefully – once again, this is another reason to practise mindfulness!

7. *Remember to recognise dates that are important to those who matter to you*
Every January, a good friend of mine writes into her new diary all the birthdays and anniversaries of everyone for whom she has that information. She writes in red ink so she notices her reminders well in advance. As a consequence, she never forgets to send a card, or to telephone her friends on dates that are important to them.

You can do the same thing electronically of course. Programme reminders into your phone to notify you of important dates a day or two in advance. If you also make it a habit to look out for cards and gifts throughout the year rather than only just before you need to send them, then you'll always have something to hand at the right time.

8. *Send a card, a funny article or a photo to someone you care about, for no other reason than to say that you're thinking about him or her*
One of my clients refers to this activity as 'sending the un-birthday presents'. Her friends love it. She told me

that they value those gestures far more than cards or gifts they receive at 'appropriate' times.

Of course, you can do this electronically rather than by hand. However, the extra time it will take you to write a message yourself and then send it by post will make the gesture seem much more special.

9. *Sign up for a class or join a group of volunteers*
This represents a bigger time commitment than any of the previous suggestions. However, it's an extremely effective way of enlarging your social support network. You'll meet some new people and you'll have an interest in common straight away. At the same time, you're giving yourself the opportunity to learn something new.

If you decide to sign up for a class, one of the best choices you can make is to learn a new language. When you learn another language you inevitably learn about another culture and other ways of living. This might awaken a desire to travel to the country where the language you're learning is spoken. If that happens, a whole range of new social opportunities will open up to you!

10. *If a relationship has stalled or is in trouble, try to find ways to work through your differences instead of simply dumping the relationship and 'moving on'*
This last suggestion is without a doubt the most important of all those that I have offered you here. This suggestion, more than any other, will help you

feel truly connected to others. Furthermore, the effort and sensitivity required of you will make you proud of yourself and raise your self-esteem.

Working hard to sort out interpersonal difficulties allows you to lead a more balanced and fulfilling life generally. Sadly, however, these days we're encouraged to be impatient and to cast aside anything that's not working perfectly. We're told to look for faults only outside ourselves. If something goes wrong between you and someone else then it must be the fault of the other person, we're told. 'You deserve better,' we're told. 'Find someone new.'

Sometimes that's correct. Most of the time, however, the causes that create problems lie with both individuals rather than just with one. If you were to take time to listen to one another, and to try to see the problem from the other person's point of view, you might well find a compromise that would smooth out your differences and allow your relationship to strengthen and deepen.

So often today, friendships and other relationships that stumble are discarded without any effort made to rescue them first. That's such a pity, because the things we work hardest to achieve are the ones we value and enjoy most. Real satisfaction and a sense of peace come only when you know you've tried your utmost with regard to what you have.

There's a song I remember that we used to sing when we were kids. It's trite but it's also wise. It goes like this:

Make new friends,
But keep the old.
For one is silver
And the other is gold.

Why a Healthy Social Life is So Important

1. Take time regularly to meet face-to-face with those who matter most to you. As a consequence you'll feel more secure and your life will have more meaning.

2. It's essential for healthy psychological development to know who you are and with whom you identify. Learn more about your family and you'll know yourself better.

3. Your life will be richer and more enjoyable when you socialise regularly with those who are important to you. This may also help to protect you from both psychological and physical illness, and there's also evidence to suggest that it may boost your immune system as well.

4. The most satisfying way to spend time with those who matter most to you is to meet up in person. Failing that, use Skype or the telephone. Use forms of remote communication (texts, emails and social networks etc.) only when other methods are not possible.

5. Look for opportunities to interact directly with someone every day. Thank or compliment another person whenever you can do so genuinely, offer help to someone less able than you, and remember dates that are important to your loved ones.

6. When a relationship is in trouble try to find ways to work through your differences. The relationships that you work hardest to maintain will be the ones that you'll value most.

A Last Word

I hope that the five steps presented in this book have given you new direction and inspiration, as they have for so many of the people I've worked with and taught over the years.

I hope, too, you now realise that you already have everything you need to live a calmer and more balanced life. There's no need to take any courses or to buy any equipment. The secret lies in your attitude to life, not in your wallet. If you take on board the suggestions in this book and determine to make one change, however small, every week, you'll be delighted with the results.

DARING TO CHANGE

Change always seems a bit daunting. It's much easier to stay in a familiar rut than it is to dare to make a change.

Yet only when you put in that effort and try something new will you really feel fully alive. You would not have picked up this book if you were utterly content with the way you're living your life. Now that you've read through the five steps, you know how to discover your gifts and talents. You've learned ways that you might express what you have to offer more effectively. You understand better how to organise yourself and set priorities that carry new meaning. You know the importance of taking care of yourself and of making time with others a priority. And most of all, you understand the need for stillness, the need to sit quietly and notice all that you have and all that is around you.

When you stumble

Notice that I said *when* you stumble not *if* you stumble. That's because not all of the changes you decide to make will turn out to be right for you, or at least not right for you forever more.

None of us can ever know exactly how we'll feel about a new way of doing something until we actually try it out. It's *not* failure to decide that you need to do something differently. That's courage. One of the many reasons why you'll benefit from mindful awareness is that you'll know when things are 'right', for you, and when it's time for a further improvement in the way you're living.

A Last Word

Now is the time.
There's never a better time to start living a richer and
fuller life than right now.

Like the child who turns her kaleidoscope and sees a completely new pattern even though the pieces of colour have remained the same, so you, too, can enjoy a happier and more fulfilling life. You already have what you need to do so.

All you need to do now is to look in new ways at who you are and at what you already have.

Acknowledgements

I am always humbled when I think about how many people have helped me write each book. Although an isolated profession in some ways, authors really owe a debt to a whole host of people who make the final product possible.

I would like to start by thanking my patients, the individuals who have come to me distressed, and trusted in me and in our work together. Each of you has taught me something valuable. Thanks to you all.

Thanks, too, to my professional team. I'd like to thank my agent Jane Turnbull and Paola Ehrlich. How did I ever, ever manage before I knew you?! Not only have you supported and believed in me wholeheartedly, but you have *always* made yourself available when I needed you. Thanks, too, to my wonderful team at Hodder: Rowena Webb, Liz Gough, Maddy Price, Ciara Foley, Emilie Ferguson, Emily

Robertson, and Sophie Camp. Maddy and Ciara, you made editing seem almost like *fun;* and the efforts you all made to encourage me and to promote my book has been unparalleled. I am just so grateful.

Finally, I want to thank my friends, colleagues and family, those who have encouraged me when I doubted, helped by listening and offering suggestions, and managed somehow to make allowances cheerfully for me when I became so absorbed that I forgot about everything else! Thanks to my brother Paul and sisters Christen and Penny, my colleagues Bill, Jack, Ruth and Nicole, and to my great friends Fiona, Frances, and Daphne. Most of all I want to say thanks to Jonathan, Sam and Katy, and to Rob, my dearest friend and love.

References

Blair, Linda. *Birth Order: What Your Position in the Family Really Tells You About Your Character.* London: Piatkus Books, 2011.

Blair, Linda. *Straight Talking.* London: Piatkus Books, 2009.

Brown, G.W., Andrews, B., Harris, T., Adler, Z. and Bridge, L. 'Social Support, Self-Esteem and Depression'. *Psychological Medicine,* November 1986, Vol. 16 No. 4, 813–831.

Bryson, Bill. *Notes From a Big Country.* London: Transworld Publishers Ltd., 1998.

Byrne, Rhonda, *The Secret.* London: Simon and Schuster UK Ltd., 2006.

Cameron, Julia. *The Artist's Way: A Course in Discovering and Recovering Your Creative Self.* London: Pan Books (Macmillan Publishers Ltd.), 1995.

Covey, Stephen R. *The 7 Habits of Highly Effective People*. London: Simon and Schuster UK Ltd., 1999.

Crenshaw, Dave. *The Myth of Multitasking*. San Francisco: Jossey-Bass (Wiley), 2008.

Csikszentmihalyi, Mihaly. *Flow: The Classic Work on How to Achieve Happiness*. London: Rider (Random House Group Ltd.), 2002.

Davis, Adelle. *Let's Eat Right to Keep Fit*. London: Unwin Paperbacks, 1979.

Donnelly, Laura. 'How Twitter Can Turn to Fluster'. *The Sunday Telegraph*, 8 July 2012, 17.

Duhigg, Charles. *The Power of Habit: Why We Do What We Do and How to Change*. London: William Heinemann, 2012.

Earle, Richard, Imrie, David and Archbold, Rick. *Your Vitality Factor*. London: Pan Books (Macmillan Publishers Ltd.), 1991.

Eysenck, H.J. and Eysenck, Sybil B.G. *Eysenck Personality Inventory*. London: University of London Press Ltd., 1969.

Gandy, Ellen. 'Four Years Ago I got Carried Away. Now I am Ready to Race'. *The Daily Telegraph*, 27 July 2012, S14.

References

Gardner, Howard. *Frames of Mind: The Theory of Multiple Intelligences*. London: Paladin Books (Granada Publishing Ltd.), 1985.

Gibran, Kahlil. *The Prophet*. London: Penguin Books Inc., 1992.

Gladwell, Malcolm. *Blink: The Power of Thinking Without Thinking*. London: Penguin Books, 2006.

Glass, Thomas A., Mendes de Leon, Carlos, Marottoli, Richard A. and Berkman, Lisa F. 'Population Based Study of Social and Productive Activities as Predictors of Survival Among Elderly Americans'. *British Medical Journal*, August 1999.

Gleitman, Henry, Gross, James, and Reisberg, Daniel. *Psychology*. New York: W.W. Norton and Co., Inc., 2011 (Eighth Edition).

Hanh, Thich Nhat. *Old Path, White Clouds*. Delhi: Full Circle, 1991.

Hanh, Thich Nhat. *The Miracle of Mindfulness*. London: Rider (Ebury Publishing), 2008.

Harrison, Theresa M., Weintraub, Sandra, Mesulam, M-Marsel and Rogalski, Emily. 'Superior Memory and Higher Cortical Volumes in Unusually Successful Cognitive Aging'. *Journal of the International Neuropsychological Society*, 2012, Vol. 18, 1–5.

Herriot, James. *It Shouldn't Happen to a Vet*. London: Pan Books (Macmillan Publishers Ltd.), 2006.

House, J.S., Landis, K.R. and Umberson, D. 'Social Relationships and Health'. *Science*, 29 July 1988, Vol. 241 No. 4865, 540–545.

Khan, Akram. Interview with Kirsty Young on 'Desert Island Discs'. BBC Radio 4, 22 July 2012.

Iyengar, S.S. and Lepper, M.R. 'When Choice is Demotivating: Can One Desire Too Much of a Good Thing?' *Journal of Personality and Social Psychology*, December 2000, Vol. 79 No. 6, 995–1006.

Kabat-Zinn, Jon. *Full Catastrophe Living*. London: Piatkus Books, 2004.

Kabat-Zinn, Jon. *Wherever You Go, There You Are*. London: Piatkus Books, 1994.

Kiecolt-Glaser, J.K., Garner, W., Speicher, C., Penn, G.M., Holliday, J. and Glaser, R. 'Psychosocial Modifiers of Immunocompetence in Medical Students'. *Psychosomatic Medicine*, 1 January 1984, Vol. 46 No. 1, 7–14.

King, Elizabeth. 'The Jam Experiment: On Choice'. Blog, 15 July 2010.

Kwei-Armah, Kwame. 'Going Back to My Roots'. *BBC News Magazine*, 23 March 2007.

Laney, Marti Olsen. *The Introvert Advantage: How to Thrive in an Extrovert World*. New York: Workman Publishing, 2002.

McHugh, Joanna E. and Lawlor, Brian A. 'Exercise and Social Support Are Associated With Psychological Distress Outcomes in a Population of Community-Dwelling Older Adults'. *Journal of Health Psychology*, September 2012, Vol. 17 No. 6, 833–844.

Puddicombe, Andy. *Get Some Headspace*. London: Hodder and Stoughton, 2011.

Reader's Digest Health Solutions, *Stay Calm Stay Healthy*. London: The Reader's Digest Association, Inc., 2011.

Redgrave, Sir Steve. 'You Are Never Forgotten as an Olympic Champion'. *Daily Telegraph*, 17 August 2012, S12.

Segal, Zindel V., Williams, J. Mark G. and Teasdale, John D. *Mindfulness-Based Cognitive Therapy for Depression*. London: The Guilford Press, 2002.

Servan-Schreiber, David. *Anticancer: A New Way of Life*. London: Penguin Books Ltd., 2007.

Smith, Rebecca. 'The Secrets Hidden in Supergran's Brain'. *Daily Telegraph*, 17 August 2012, 3.

Tolstoy, Leo. *Twenty-three Tales*. New York: Funk and Wagnalls Co., 1907.

Van Straten, Michael and Griggs, Barbara. *Superfoods.* London: Dorling Kindersley, 1990.

Williams, Mark and Penman, Danny. *Mindfulness: A Practical Guide to Finding Peace in a Frantic World.* London: Piatkus, 2011.

Wolesley, Pat. Interview with Jim Al-Khalili on 'The Life Scientific'. BBC Radio 4, 14 August 2012.

yellow kite

books to help you live a good life

Join the conversation and tell
us how you live a #goodlife

🐦 @yellowkitebooks

f YellowKiteBooks

P Yellow Kite Books

📷 YellowKiteBooks